Getting the Buggers to Draw

Barbara Ward

continuum
LONDON • NEW YORK

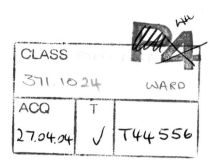
Continuum International Publishing Group
The Tower Building   15 East 26th Street
11 York Road   New York
London SE1 7NX   NY 10010

www.continuumbooks.com

First published 2003 by Continuum

British Library Cataloguing-in-Publication Data
A catalogue record for this book is available from the British Library

ISBN 0-8264-6929-9 (paperback)

Typeset by Kenneth Burnley, Wirral, Cheshire
Printed and bound in Great Britain

Contents

List of Figures

Acknowledgements

To Maurice for his endless patience and constant support. To Sue Holland and the Junior staff of Ladybridge Primary School who allowed me to experiment with the curriculum, who encouraged me to carry on against all adversities and especially to the heads, teachers and children in the schools that have helped me to prove that this system works. To the pleasure of seeing all those happy faces when they found out they could do such lovely work!

This book is dedicated to you all, so that children all over the world can find the joy of being able to draw.

Preface

Are you one of those people who have no confidence in their own drawing ability, let alone the confidence needed to instruct children on how to draw the basic shapes around them?

With the aid of this book you will be able to hone your own observational skills and teach 'guided' drawing to the children. It will give you all a greater sense of satisfaction because most people, especially children, love to be able to 'draw properly'.

It is wonderful to get feedback such as 'I'm teaching my mum to draw now', 'I've been drawing at home' and 'Do we have to go out to play?' I have held classes for grannies also and have watched with much pleasure the way they have shown off their new-found skills to their offspring.

This book on guided drawing is not intended to be read cover to cover, but as a visual dictionary to be used as necessary. Remember that there are no hard and fast rules, or age-attainment targets, as it is a natural progression. The methods and techniques shown here can be used whenever you feel that the children you teach are ready for them.

This book enables you as the teacher to stay one step ahead of the children without hours of research and preparation. It will give you a new confidence in your own drawing ability and the children will be given a chance to develop their visual awareness and manipulative skills to the full.

I dream of a day when nobody feels the need to say 'I can't draw'. Everybody has the ability to draw; they just haven't received the same level of guidance, or had as much experience.

It has worked for me – it can work for you. Enjoy!

1 Starting Points

1 Why is art so important?

Art is an international form of communication dealing with the natural world at an emotional level, a basic common skill that passes beyond the barriers of culture, language and creed. It conveys innermost emotions from the primitive to the sophisticated man and his environment. The caveman knew this better than modern man: he was unable to leave us any written word, nevertheless he gave us a timeless legacy in the animals and hunting scenes that feature in cave paintings.

Drawing is used by many professionals to allow otherwise uncommunicative people to make acceptable emotional statements, where language would be completely inadequate. As a means of communication that needs no written or spoken word it can break through emotional, racial and cultural barriers.

Drawing is not, however, just a specialist subject for the elite; it is instead an important part of a child's development, just as it was a hundred years ago. Its rules and presentation are most nearly related to the rules of mathematics because its guidelines and progression are logical. It is one of the building-blocks of life.

As a cornerstone in education, drawing teaches the ability to convert theoretical progression into practicality. It plays a significant part in recognition, identification and relationships in each and every interactive subject. All children now have numeracy and literacy periods every day. Why not give them the chance to do even better in all subjects? Which subject would not benefit from an enhanced visual memory and better observational skills?

Creating works of significance, or indeed of beauty, stimulates joy and excitement, and in its creation can bring peace and tranquillity, and most importantly a sense of achievement. There are many children who find the written word frustratingly hard, and as a result become disaffected and disruptive. Drawing, it has been proved, helps in these cases.

Is it really of any use?

The ability to look, see and understand will benefit the students during the whole of their development, in every area of the curriculum. Recognition of what they see, and describing or making a representation of it on paper with confidence, is a skill that needs to be taught. Without this, how can they describe a scene, draw with more confidence or present the necessary diagrams and details in other subjects, so that they can be of use later on?

If all children were trained to look at everyday objects (or in the case of adults, to look more carefully), to 'see' and recognize and understand what they see, they would find it easier to draw. There would be less frustration, increasing confidence, greater satisfaction and a sense of real achievement. There would be less of the 'I can't', and more of the 'It's a bit like the shape of a . . .'.

These days primary school children are learning so many subjects; however, the experience most missing is surely the one of 'seeing'. The clarity of perception is the basis of understanding, and practice is the answer to all problems in the visual world. Given practice, which I know is not easy, with so many subjects to cover, their 'green activity' of art can be far more productive. 'Go and paint a picture', or 'Illustrate that story' and 'That's lovely, put it over there to dry', in no way encourages a child to improve its observational skills or drawing ability.

Teaching the all-embracing concept of visual awareness cannot be started too soon. An infant has a fantastic sponge of a brain which is open to new ideas and able to absorb new concepts far more easily than, say, a 10-year-old, who, even at that age, is already set in his views about whether he can or can't do something.

Most primary school children aged 6 or more have a rough-book, a busy-book or draft-book. Should every day start with a short numeracy test, or could one day a week perhaps be an 'observation' session? A 'busy-book' in the infants' school could be useful for drawing practice before school as well as a place to do handwriting.

You can't drive a car without learning hand and eye coordination, so why should a child be expected to draw an object or person without tuition and practice? How many adults can draw a human figure unless they have been to art school? Not too many, but why shouldn't everyone learn the basics?

2 The motivation to draw

Improved observation

Perception in most people is greater than their ability to see. Unless we have trained ourselves, we look at an object with only a slightly advanced version of 'concrete thought'. A cube has six sides, but how many can we see at any one time? It is not what you *know* you are looking at, but what you can *actually see* that matters.

For most artists drawing is not an inherited skill. They have just learned the basic rules and observed their environment more carefully. Good drawing is 80 per cent based on observation and only 20 per cent skill. Children can be trained to look at shapes, while adults can learn to look more carefully. Drawing is a logical mathematical progression. Learn the simple rules and you will see and understand, rather than just looking at objects around you.

Building confidence

Give yourself the chance to improve your own skills by using the tools of the art student. There is no set time-scale for learning to draw well. To teach drawing, all you need to do is to keep yourself one step ahead of the class, so that you can demonstrate a shape or shadow to them on the board.

At any available moment, instead of doodling, you can practise an object or some shading, familiarizing yourself with a shape that you have not drawn before. A cube is most people's favourite, but do try one of the others. We can all improve, no matter how good we think we are. Your own eyes will tell you whether it looks right or nearly right.

Better presentation of work

Teachers in primary schools, who have to cover all the subjects in the curriculum, find that there are many times when they have to demonstrate and draw on the board. Science diagrams are often particularly taxing to the less confident. Think how much easier it would be if you had more confidence in your own drawing ability!

Build up your own confidence first, and then try out simple drawing lessons in class. You will find that being able to demonstrate a competent drawing or diagram will give your class the chance to achieve a far better standard of presentation. They need to see a good adult drawing, otherwise they have no standard at which to aim.

An interested class

We all know that there is nothing more enjoyable than teaching a keen and interested class. They love drawing once they can see an improvement in their own skills and look forward to their next session. They can have a real sense of achievement, with your help, after only one guided lesson. Their enhanced drawing skills will be an asset in any subjects that require illustrations, maps or diagrams, and the presentation of their work will show a marked improvement.

Sense of achievement

Drawing classes bring out the best in the most unlikely children. Often, previously disruptive or statemented children, who many times feel out of it, find that their work is just as good as – or even better than – that of their peers. This is a subject that crosses barriers and can give both you and the class a real sense of achievement.

I am in no way doubting your ability, but I am going to assume that drawing does not come naturally to you. I will take you through each step, as I would with any student beginner who has had no drawing lessons before. You can then use the methods here to teach your own class, making the necessary adaptations for age and ability.

3 What are the basics?

Pencils

Which pencils do we need to achieve the right shading tone?

Drawing pencils are much softer than writing pencils and range from B to 9B. Writing pencils are usually HB and need pressure to mark the paper. School drawing pencils are usually 2–3B and need a lighter touch than you may realize. If not used that way they cannot be erased and tend to smudge, especially if you rub your hand across the paper. You need this soft effect sometimes with shading, to make a surface look smooth, but children tend to smudge the whole page without meaning to, and in a sketchbook it can spoil the opposite page as well.

Paper

Cartridge/drawing paper is used by artists and architects alike and is expensive, but you don't need to use it all the time. On the rougher paper it is more difficult to produce softer shading. Sketchbooks have slightly rougher paper, so need a lighter pressure on the pencil than you would apply with writing. Photocopy paper is quite adequate for most drawing, but needs more pressure for dark shading. This is difficult to erase and the paper often creases if not held carefully on either side. Schools usually have 'drawing paper', which is excellent for the work we are going to tackle here.

Erasers

You do need a softer eraser for rubbing out lines made with soft drawing pencils. Normal cheap school erasers are often far from adequate. Check the ones you have in the classroom to make sure they work properly. They can look fantastic on day one, but ruin the work as soon they are used. Hi-polymer erasers are ideal for all types of pencil-work. They erase both soft and hard pencils, and for the price of one eraser to four children you can have good presentation of exercise-books and drawings. A small price to pay for neat work!

Fixative
Fixative prevents smudging, but is expensive. A cheap hairspray is almost as good and quite sufficient for most purposes. It is essential when drawing with soft pencils, charcoal, chalk and some pastels.

4 Tones and textures

Tones of the pencil
We need to understand the many different colours (tones) that can be achieved by a single pencil.

(a) Using first the writing pencil, draw a set of squares across a piece of paper (see Figure 1.1a). Fill them in with gradually darkening shades of grey. The lightest tone should be hardly visible.
(b) Repeat this with a 2B pencil (Figure 1.1b) and you will immediately see the difference. The light tones are more difficult to obtain and the darker ones easier because they need far less pressure.
(c) If you then use a 9B pencil (Figure 1.1c) the black is thick and rich and the palest tone is very difficult to produce. Try not to rub over the squares because smudging these squares is too easily done and the hands get very dirty.
(d) Cross hatching is a method for dark shading (see Chapter 3, p. 29).

Textures
If you were doing a drawing of a child with a teddy-bear, you would need to have some way of showing the difference between the child's hair and the fur of the bear.

When a surface is not smooth and it is necessary to show what it looks like to complete the effect, then a texture can be added. Textures are very small, all-over patterns that suggest rather than copy the surface of the object. Make the patterns too large and they become a pattern, not a texture.

Shading is a texture, but is usually smooth. Rough shading makes the flat face of an object look lumpy, but there are many other ways to change the finished effect.

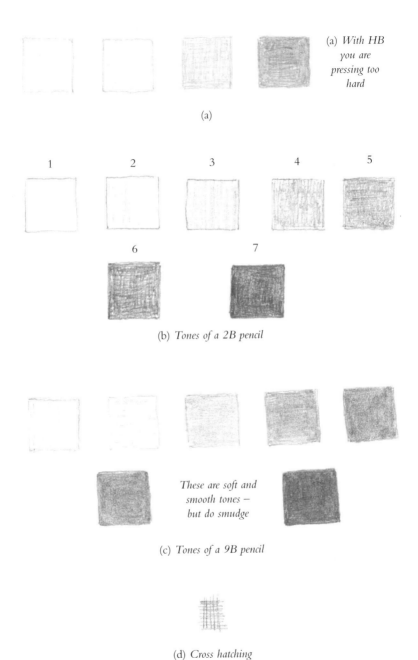

(a) *With HB you are pressing too hard*

(a)

(b) *Tones of a 2B pencil*

These are soft and smooth tones – but do smudge

(c) *Tones of a 9B pencil*

(d) *Cross hatching*

Figure 1.1: Tones of different pencils

Crosshatching is a series of fine lines almost at right angles to each other (see Figure 1.1d). Double lines across in one direction look like corduroy or stripes, while tiny dots close together can portray anything from the centre of a daisy to the stubble on a person's chin. The short hairstyles of boys today can best be shown with small zigzags or short lines close together.

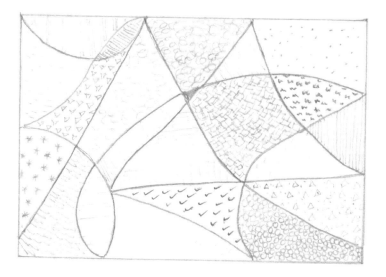

Figure 1.2: Textures

Textures can be done in pencil or any single colour, flat on the surface or scraped into thick paint. Many textures together can be made into a pattern, as in Figure 1.2. This can be a good exercise to reinforce texture as opposed to pattern, and makes an excellent display when done by a class. Each one suggests a different 'feel': rough, smooth, lumpy, soft or ridged.

On a sheet of A4 paper, draw a large scribble that reaches the edges in several places, as in Figure 1.2, and fill in the spaces with types of texture, making sure that the adjacent shapes have different depths of colour, dark next to light, large next to small. It can be done in any drawing media or with a fine brush. Each one suggests a different 'feel' or texture.

Remember to try this out on a class when you have a spare moment.

5 Sketching techniques

Changing the grip on the pencil

When we are writing we rest the heel or side of the hand on the paper (see Figure 1.3a). When drawing we need more space and leverage than for writing, so we have to rest the wrist or base of the little finger on the paper, depending on the amount of paper we need to cover in one movement of the pencil.

Learn to relax the grip on the pencil so that you can 'sketch' rather than draw. Move the point of the pencil 2–3 cms further away from your fingertips and try to straighten your fingers slightly. This softens your grip on the tip of the pencil (see Figure 1.3b). This means that you can draw several soft lines when starting, and then later go over the one you prefer. The light sketch-lines can form part of the finished drawing, giving a soft edge which can enhance the effect and give it a freshness that one careful line does not. However, if need be, soft lines are more easily erased than stronger lines.

If you rest your wrist on the paper and use that as a centre, or fulcrum, you will find that you can draw a large curved shape. Rest your little finger on the paper and you can describe a smaller curve. With the first knuckle of the little finger on the paper, the curve is smaller still.

If straight lines are required for shading, the hand has to lift off the paper altogether. Practise straight lines very softly, horizontally and vertically, as this will be essential. If either is more difficult, you can always turn the drawing round through 90 degrees. Unfortunately it is impossible to turn a board round when you are demonstrating to a class!

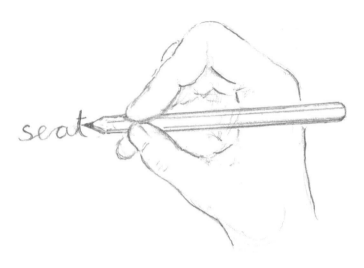

(a) *Usual writing position*

(b) *Sketching position: making a softer line that is easier to erase*

Figure 1.3: Sketching

2 Learning to Look

1 A startling way to begin: portraits

This chapter will, I hope, show you almost immediately that with just a little help it *is* possible to draw.

All children have at some time tried to draw faces, and since this needs no elaborate artistic materials it is a very satisfying way to start any drawing session because the end results are so worthwhile. However, before starting or looking at the following pages, take a piece of spare paper and draw a face. This is to give you the 'before and after' experience of guided drawing.

Now take a clean sheet of drawing paper and read on.

The shape of the head

- The shape of the head is important to start with. Children usually think it is a circle (sphere), but in reality it is another geometric shape: an oval (egg-shape). From the front it is a rounded egg and from the side a pointed egg because of the chin.
- Set out the page so that the head is in the top two-thirds of it. Use soft curves on each side, as in the sketching technique, and smaller curves, top and bottom, turning the paper round to make it easier.
- It really does not matter exactly what shape egg you draw. It is bound to look correct, because all heads are slightly different. It will have a character of its own. (Note, it is almost impossible to draw the same shape twice!)

Proportions of the head

(a) Divide the head lightly into four, horizontally and vertically, using faint dotted lines (see Figure 2.1).

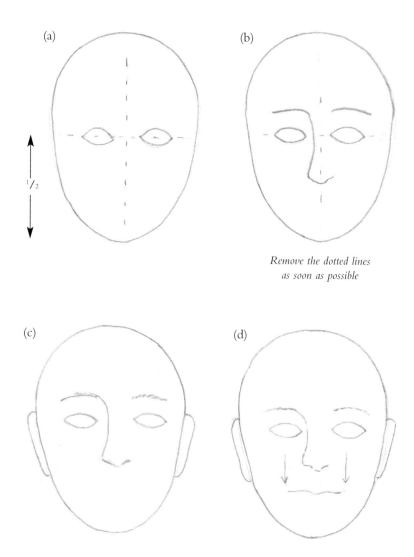

(a)

(b)

$^1/_2$

Remove the dotted lines
as soon as possible

(c)

(d)

Figure 2.1: Proportions of the head

Eyes are almond-shaped and on average they are half-way down the head, so draw in two shapes on the horizontal line, one eye apart.

The nose and eyebrows
Look for the shading on any face. There are no lines down the side of the nose to distinguish the nose from the cheeks, but there is shadow on one side to suggest the difference. Early religious paintings show us the best and easiest way to show the nose as a soft line down one side. A typical nose reaches almost half-way down from the eyes towards the chin. (See p. 14 on noses.)

(b) Take a soft line from above the eye on one side. Curve it towards the centre, not as far as the centre line, then down and slightly outwards, making a shallow V at the base. You can now erase the dotted lines before continuing.

   Add a similar curve above the other eye for the other eyebrow.

(c) Thicken the eyebrows with more hair, with short lines upwards and outwards, and emphasize the nostrils with slight upward curves. Add the ears, like two thin slices of apple, from about the eyes (spectacle arms stay about level) down just below the nose.

(d) Suggest, rather than draw, where the lips meet, with a curved line, rather like a horizontal cupid's bow. It should reach to about the centre of the eyes above and be half-way between nose and chin.

There are many differently shaped noses and mouths (see Figure 2.2). Each shows an individual characteristic. It is rather like mix-and-match clothes: put any two together and you have a 'new look'.

The lips
There is no line around the mouth and we are not concerned with anything here but shadow.

(a) The top lip curves in towards the mouth-line and most of it is in shadow. We are doing a pencil-drawing of light and

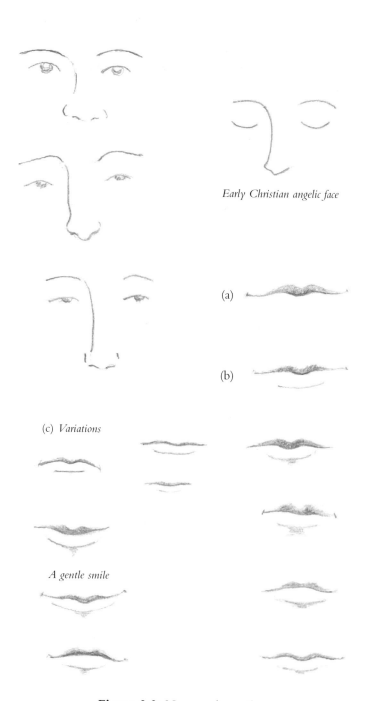

Early Christian angelic face

(a)

(b)

(c) Variations

A gentle smile

Figure 2.2: Noses and mouths

shade, so we show the shadow of the lip not the colour of it. Make a bow-shape of very soft shading for that curve, as shown, and add a small line at each end for the curve of the cheek.

(b) The bottom lip curves outwards and is in full light, so it cannot be shaded. Only the shadow below it gives the shape and it doesn't reach the outer ends of the mouth. This shadow can be just a line or it can be deeper in the centre if the chin is very pronounced. (See the variations in (c).)

The hair

The hair covers the top quarter of the head and of course spreads outside the line of the head depending on the hairstyle (see Figure 2.3, a and b). If more hair is added above the outline of the head the face looks younger because children's faces are not fully developed and their eyes are below half-way down the face as in (c).

There is no need to show every hair, but making curves, small zigzags or scribbles for tight curls can give good representations of different styles.

The neck is a cylinder (d) that fits onto the front of the body. It starts at about mouth-level and curves out slightly at the base. The necklace line shows the curve of the elliptical base.

The shoulders slope from behind the neck and not to the side of it. They are about two heads' widths across and can be suggested rather than drawn.

Completing the eyes

The eyes are the most interesting and expressive part of the face and are best left till last. (See Figure 2.4 for stages in drawing the eyes.)

(ai) Check that the eyes are correct, in that they are oval or almond-shaped and the correct distance apart. If the oval is too deep then add another line inside, at the top to make an eyelid (aii).

(b) The iris is circular, but how often can we see the whole shape? Only when a person is surprised or afraid. Part of the circle is behind the eyelid. Draw two circles that are too big to complete and are hidden top and bottom behind the lids. Add the part-eyelid if it wasn't done before.

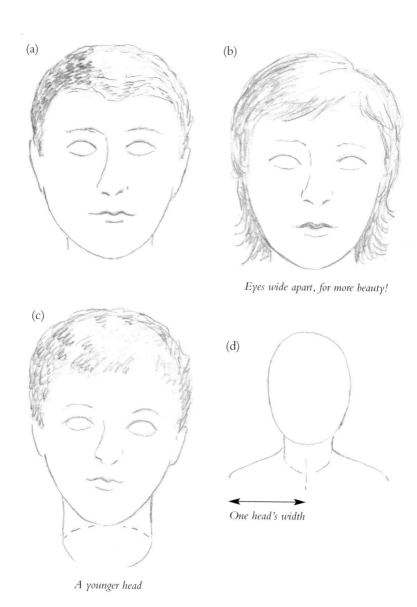

(a)

(b)

Eyes wide apart, for more beauty!

(c)

(d)

One head's width

A younger head

Figure 2.3: The hair

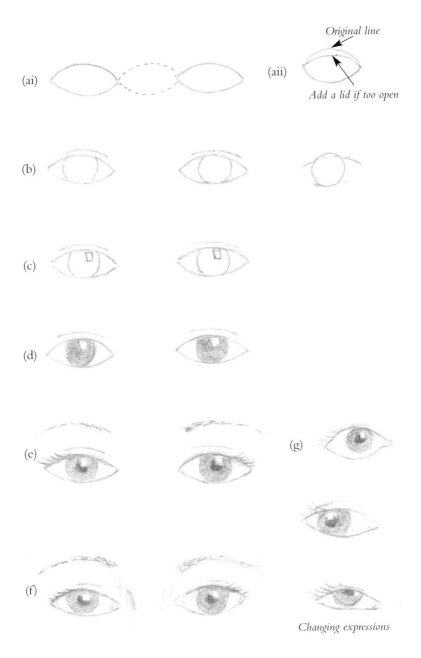

(ai)

(aii)

Original line

Add a lid if too open

(b)

(c)

(d)

(e)

(g)

(f)

Changing expressions

Figure 2.4: The eyes

(c) All eyes have a reflection in them, from the light source. This is what makes them look alive, so draw a small square, in the same place in each of the eyes, for the reflection.

(d) Shade in the rest of the iris, making sure that the little square stays white.

(e) Add a fairly large pupil partly cut off by the reflection. Emphasize the top lid with a stronger line and a *few* eyelashes on the outer quarter of the lid only. (More than a few make it look like a clown!) Check that the eyebrows are slightly thicker towards the nose.

(f) Shade very lightly round the side of the nose area, more on the shadow side. Also add a slight shade at each end of the eyeball itself to make it look solid.

(g) By moving the iris up, down or out and closing the shape of the oval, you can get many different expressions. Always put the iris in the same part of each eye, so that they correspond with each other, or the face will look cross-eyed.

Completing the portrait

Completing the portrait with a collar or neckline is not really important, but the neck is a cylinder and the clothes, collars or neckline must fit round it (see Figure 2.5).

Drawing is not about completing a whole page. It is about making a good representation of part of what you see. It could be just the eyes or the face without the hair. Often a picture looks better if it just fades away towards the outside because it suggests rather than shows. You want an observer to look at the face, not the make of the clothes!

Keep any extras to the minimum and they will be pleasing to the eye. Collars and necklines have to fit the shape of the wearer and these sketches are slight suggestions of simple finishing touches. The shading can be very sketchy, curved round the jaw and neck, diagonal on the larger areas (see Figure 2.5a).

When you are drawing a particular person's portrait you have to look carefully at the features and compare them with this 'bland' portrait. The shape of the head differs from one person to another. Small children have small faces and large tops to their heads. Look for square faces, round chins, pointed chins, shorter noses, fuller lips and straighter eyebrows. There are so

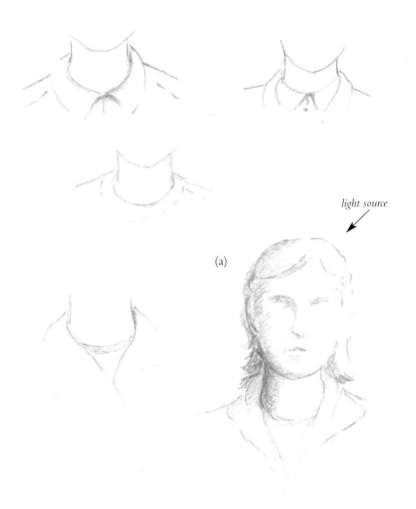

(a)

light source

Figure 2.5: Completing the portrait

many variations in the human race – each face is remarkably individual.

I do hope that you like your first portrait. Try doing some more: each one will be completely different – all little individuals! (See Chapter 10 for portraits done in the first session by 7–year–olds.)

2 Why looking is so important

Without looking carefully we are unable to see the exact shape of an object. The more you practise and the more you look, the better the drawing. We can improve our observation skills by using what the artists have used to help them get the shape and proportion correct. We ourselves may not be accomplished artists, but it really does help, as in any other subject, if we use the right tools.

3 Making and using the frames

A benchmark

When we are looking at shapes and angles we need a 'benchmark' to work from, or we cannot see the angles and curves of an object. (See QCA, 'the viewfinder'.) A rectangular shape gives us square corners and straight sides, so that we can compare them with the shapes and angles we are looking at.

These are the 'tools' of the artist and art student, in order to get the shape and proportion of something without the distracting surroundings, so why can't we all use them? With these we can see the shapes in front of us, the angles and curves, far more clearly than if we just look with our eyes.

Take half a sheet of A4 paper or thin card and follow the diagrams to make two shaped frames (see Figure 2.6).

Cut out the centre section carefully so that you have good right-angle corners. Label the long side 'landscape' and the short side 'portrait'.

The rectangular frame

Get used to looking through the rectangular frame and you can start to <u>see</u> the shapes and angles in everyday life. When you start

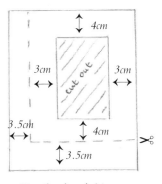

Two 'benchmarks' in one
Half a sheet of A4

Hold the frame vertical in 'portrait'
to observe objects carefully

Figure 2.6: Making the frame and right-angle guide

your observation, make sure you are holding the frame vertically by lining up the frame with something you know to be vertical, and then gently move it sideways so that the object you want to observe is in the centre of the frame. Providing you hold the frame level, you can check both the horizontal and vertical of anything.

Closing one eye, you can line up any object in the centre and look at it really carefully. Move the frame closer to your face for a long view, and towards the object for a close-up of the detail. Move the frame until it seems to touch one side of the object, then move it up until it 'touches' the base of the object too. The shape of the space around the object is just as important as its own shape and will help you to draw it.

This frame will help you to observe carefully a whole garden scene or a single flower, a whole room or a single fold in a piece of fabric. By moving the edge of the frame to 'touch' the shapes, it is easy to see the angles of each section.

The L-shaped frame

The L-shape must be held up with one side absolutely vertical. If marked off in segments, as in Figure 2.7, it will be most useful for gauging the height and width of a single object, or group of objects, or for observing the height of a steeple compared with the

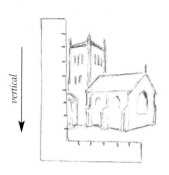

vertical

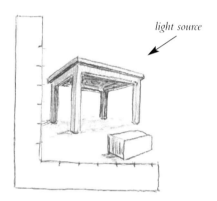

light source

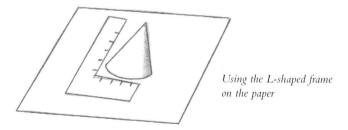

Using the L-shaped frame on the paper

Figure 2.7: The L-shaped frame

width of the church. You can 'measure' things with your eye, like the number of times a person's head fits into their height, or how wide the shoulders are compared with the head. For small objects you can even lay it down on the paper to mark off the 'touching' points, if you want to be very accurate.

The plumb-line

This is the tool of art students who are used to observing objects. When you have had some practice, the plumb-line is useful for gauging verticals only. If you want to find the vertical edges of any object, tie a rubber on to some fine thread and hold it up. (See Figure 2.8.) It makes a perfect vertical. Close one eye and view the object. Hold the plumb-line next to one corner or side of any object you wish to observe. You can then move it across horizontally to find all the verticals. As you grow more confident you may find that this is the only benchmark you need.

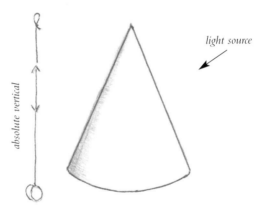

Figure 2.8: The plumb-line

4 Light and shade

Pencil-drawings are made up entirely of line and tone, light and shade.

Think of any shape you know well, not as a mathematical diagram but as a study in light and shade. The background is as important as the object. See familiar shapes in this new way and understand the logical sequence towards drawing skills. Half close your eyes and look only for light and dark and the world will take on a whole new angle, a patchwork of light and shade. You are going to draw what you *see* and not what you *know* is there.

Two-dimensional (2D) shapes cut out and laid flat have a very tiny shadow but 3D shapes have very distinct shadows. This light and shade on an object is the only way of showing a 3D shape in a 2D drawing (see Figure 2.9).

You can see a snowball sitting in the snow because it casts a shadow. Could we see it when it is dark? No, we need light shining on it, reflected into our eyes.

Place a cube on a piece of paper the same colour. It shows up quite clearly on one side where there is a shadow, but on the other side it appears lighter than the background. This is because, as a colour recedes, it becomes less intense, so the cube looks brighter than the paper behind it.

If the light in the room is diffused and the shaded side is not so clear, then shine a lamp or strong torch on to the cube from one side. A low light makes long, diffused shadows visible on the opposite side. A high light makes very short, dark shadows clearly visible.

Shadows are more difficult to see on textured surfaces such as the bark of a tree, but with your eyes half-shut you have a 100 per cent better view, as the colour and texture become so much less important.

When we are drawing solid shapes we have to establish where the light source is, and the rest is a mathematical progression because it is logical. Follow the line of its direction. The shadow is always directly opposite. If there is more than one light source there will be more than one shadow. Try not to use shiny shapes because there will be reflections as well as shadows with which to contend.

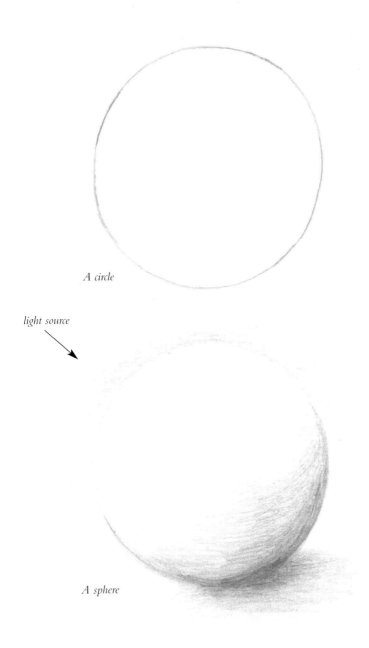

A circle

light source

A sphere

Figure 2.9: The difference between 2D and 3D shapes

3 Using Shapes to Begin Drawing

1 The cube

This is the first of the three basic shapes in the world. They are flat, flat and curved, and curved only, and remember that this is 80 per cent observation and only 20 per cent skill.

How many sides has a cube got? Six, but how many sides can you actually *see* at any one time? Two if you look straight at one side but three the rest of the time. Held up in the air or down on the table it still only shows three.

In order to draw a cube you will need a piece of paper and two pencils (an HB and a 2B), a cube and a piece of paper the same colour as the cube.

Place the cube on the piece of paper, then half close your eyes.

Using the frame in 'portrait' (see Figure 3.1) look carefully at the cube. Move the frame forward so that the cube almost fills the frame-opening. The sides of the cube are vertical, so line the frame up with them.

Now move the frame till it looks as if it touches the base of the cube. You know that all the base is flat on the table, but what shape does it look now? It has become a V shape. Do any of the right angles still look like right angles? No.

Now bring the frame up towards the face a little to show the shadow as well. That is the shape it should look on the paper when you start drawing.

Look to see which side the light is coming from (the light source) on to the shape. Look for the light side of the cube, as that should stay white on your paper when you draw it. If you can't see the shadow, then use a brighter light.

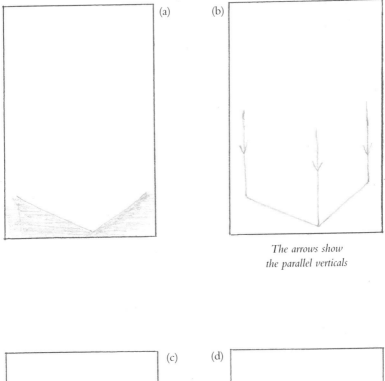

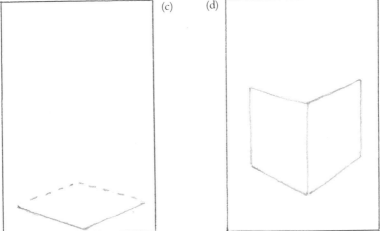

(a)　(b)

*The arrows show
the parallel verticals*

(c)　(d)

Figure 3.1: Drawing the cube looking through the frame

(a) Keeping in mind how big the cube should be on the paper, go back to the close-up view with the frame and, using the HB pencil, draw the shape of the V on to the paper so that it only just shows up. If you look at the shape of the paper below the V it will help you to draw the correct angle.

(b) Now you can draw the three verticals, the middle one slightly longer than the others.

(c) Next, hold the frame to look at the top of the cube and you will see another V, but this time it is a little shallower than at the base.

(d) When this is drawn in, the shape should look like an open book.

In order to complete the cube, you need to do the following (see Figure 3.2):

(a) Look carefully at the top of the cube and you will see a very narrow 'diamond' shape. Draw it in with the top point slightly to the side and not immediately above the lower one. (When it looks right it is!) Make all the lines darker if you are satisfied with the shape.

(b) Draw in the arrow showing the direction the light is coming from (the light source).
Using the 2B pencil, colour in the dark side of the cube, but do it vertically and then crosshatch by turning the paper round and shading over it in the direction of the cube base. This can be done in four stages as shown (see Figure 3.2b) turning the page round as you go, and emphasizes the direction in which that face is receding.

(c) The second vertical side of the cube has very light vertical shading using the HB pencil to emphasize the vertical plane or side.
Shade in the shadow on the paper, as a parallelogram of slanting lines, sloping very slightly away from the light source.

Note that all flat surfaces should be shaded very slightly in the direction of the light source. Shading that slopes too much will make a flat surface look like a slope.

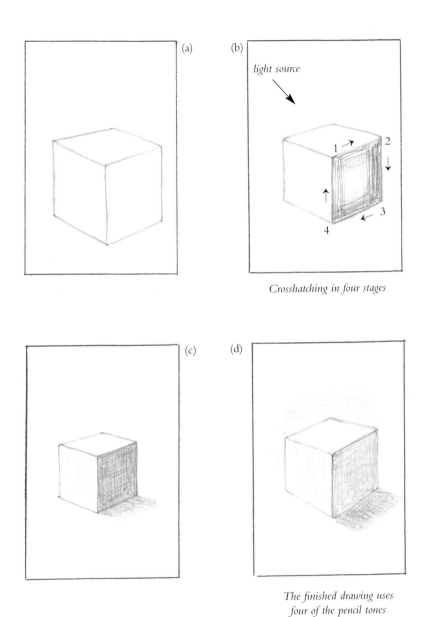

(a)

(b)

light source

1

2

3

4

Crosshatching in four stages

(c)

(d)

*The finished drawing uses
four of the pencil tones*

Figure 3.2: Completing the cube

(d) To complete the solid effect of the drawing you need to use the HB pencil again and shade in the background all around, a little paler as you come down the paper. It should be as horizontal and as smooth as you can possibly make it so that it doesn't detract from but merely highlights the white top of the cube. (See the section below on the secret of background shading.)

Move back and half close your eyes. Does it look like a solid cube? Could it be better with a little more practice? Maybe, so have another go by yourself without any reference to the above. Practice makes perfect.

This may all seem very complicated to begin with, but the following principles apply to all your drawings and, once remembered, will enhance all your work:

- Get the angles correct.
- Shade in the direction of the surface.
- To make the object look absolutely solid, shade in the background.

The secret of background shading

Background shading should be as horizontal and even as possible, if you want it to look some distance behind the object. Sky is better shaded this way as well. For accurate background shading, see Figure 3.3:

(a) Where there is a straight side it is easy to shade next to it if you mask it off with a ruler or narrow piece of paper. Turn the drawing upside down and position the ruler so that your pencil stops *on* the line and not past it. Remember to shade more lightly at the *top* because it is now upside down. (If you haven't masked it off properly there will be a slight gap and if the ruler is too wide it is more difficult to position it properly.)

(b) Move the ruler to mask off the second side and continue the shading, keeping it as horizontal as possible.

(c) Repeat this with the third side.

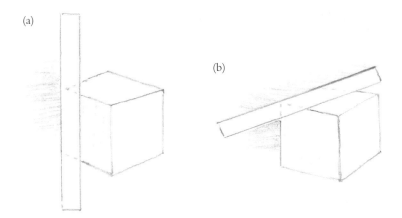

(a)

(b)

Using a ruler or a piece of paper to stop the back-ground from going on the edge of the cube

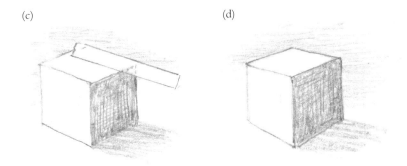

(c)

(d)

Figure 3.3: Background shading

(d) The fourth, dark side can be shaded without the masking because it is already darker than your shading, and the overlap will not show.

The paler the original drawing of the shape, the more spectacular the finished drawing!

If you sit at a table the viewpoint is lower than if you sit on a high stool (see Figure 3.4). The shape of the diamond on top of the cube shows this quite clearly.

light source

side of paper

Lower viewpoint

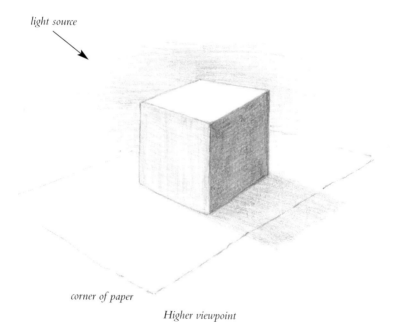

light source

corner of paper

Higher viewpoint

Figure 3.4: Lower and higher viewpoints of the cube

2 A circle in perspective

This is a very important concept because it applies to all circular shapes, round tables, archways and wheels that are turned away from the viewer.

A circle fits exactly into a square, touching the centre of each side (see Figure 3.5).

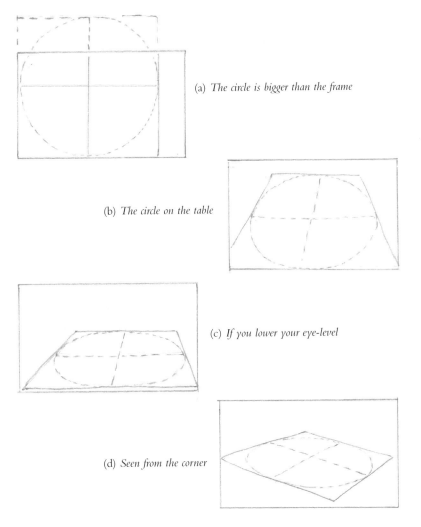

(a) *The circle is bigger than the frame*

(b) *The circle on the table*

(c) *If you lower your eye-level*

(d) *Seen from the corner*

Figure 3.5: A circle in perspective is an ellipse

(a) Draw a circle and a square around it, as in the diagram. Hold it up behind the opening in the frame. It is much larger than the opening in the frame.

(b) Lay the circle on the table and look through the frame. Immediately it is further away and in perspective, so that it 'fits' into the opening. A circle in perspective is an ellipse.

(c) If you lower your eye-level then the circle is an even shallower ellipse.

Whichever way you turn the paper, the circle stays the same shape, unless the eye-level is changed.

(d) Shows you what the circle looks like from the corner of the square.

3 The cylinder

This is the second basic shape. It has flat and curved surfaces (see Figure 3.6).

Place a pencil-pot or empty tin, covered in paper, upside down on a surface the same colour. The cylinder looks the same from every side, so it doesn't matter where you sit to view it.

Observation before drawing

(a) Looking through the frame, in portrait, you can see two straight sides and the top ellipse. The base, which you know is flat on the table, now looks like a curve. That too is part of an ellipse, but a much deeper ellipse because it is further below your eye-level, even though the cylinder may be only 5 inches deep.

(b) If you raise your eye-level by standing up, the top becomes a wide ellipse, but if you look carefully the base has become an even wider one.

(c) If you lift up the cylinder so that the top is at eye-level, the top becomes one flat line and the base is now a very shallow curve.

(d) If lifted a little higher still, you now have two curves: the top curves down and the base curves up. Both curves are equidistant from your eyes, so the curves are the same.

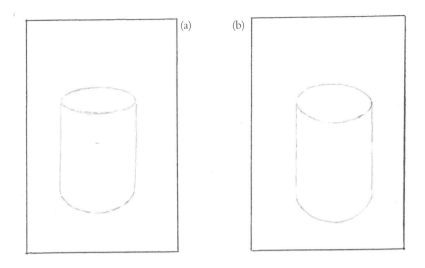

(a)   (b)

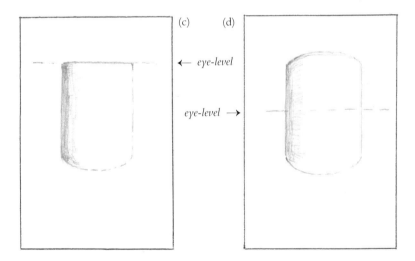

(c)   (d)

← *eye-level*

eye-level →

Figure 3.6: Observation of the cylinder: what happens to the ellipse

Drawing the cylinder

You could try this with just the drawing pencil, keeping the first lines tentative and soft until you can see that they are in the right place (see Figure 3.7). This can be drawn on the paper in portrait or landscape, but make sure there is room on the paper to show the shadow as well as the shape. See if you can draw in the paper it is sitting on as well.

(a) Draw in the two vertical parallel lines for the sides.
(b) Holding the frame so that the base curve is just above the bottom of it, look at the amount of curvature in the bottom of the cylinder. The shape of the space around it will help you. Draw in the curve so that the ends touch the sides. (This is quite difficult the first time for anyone.)
(c) Lift up the frame to compare the base curve with the top ellipse. It is difficult to see the difference between the two, but this shape is thinner and flatter than the curve of the base. To be correct and look right it has to be level and not at an angle as shown above the correct angle.
(d) Look for the light source and shadow. Shade in the shadow as it appears on the table and a few vertical lines of shading on the dark vertical side of the cylinder. This is to start off the curved shading that you need to emphasize the curve of the vertical face.

Complete the drawing with background shading as before. Only one side and the top need masking off with paper. Masking off a curved shape is a little more difficult as the ruler or paper has to be moved as you shade it.

Curved shading

Curved shading can be done in several stages (see Figure 3.8).

•   Start at the edge of the shape with a few vertical lines follow-ing the edge. It is easier to finish the edge neatly this way as it 'masks off' the curved shading from the background.
•   Turn the paper round and using the side of the hand, little finger knuckle as the pivot, make the first short dark section

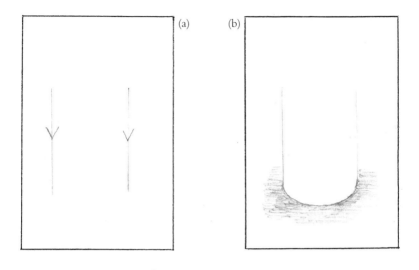

(a)   (b)

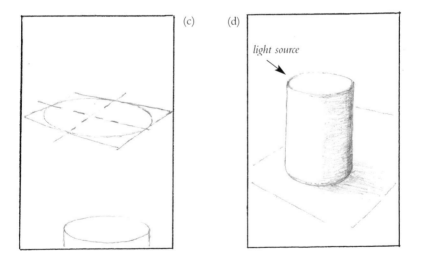

(c)   (d)

light source

Figure 3.7: Drawing the cylinder

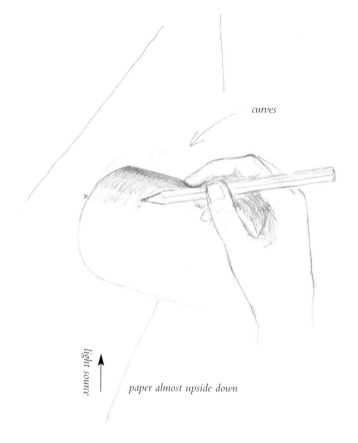

curves

light source

paper almost upside down

Figure 3.8: Curved shading made easy

of curves, moving up as you go until you have one section finished all the way up.

• Go back to the base, alter your position so that you can do the next section, and lift your pencil to make softer strokes. The smoother the shading, the better the end result.

• A third section has to be lighter again. The shadow on the paper below the cylinder, and the curved shading, has to meet at the same point (x) which may be less than in the drawing or even more depending on the direction of your light. This is because if the shadow is on the paper, there will be no light on that part of the cylinder.

4 The sphere

This is the third of the three basic shapes. It is like the cylinder, in that it looks the same from all directions and the same curved shading is used for the shadow side. If you look carefully at the shadow on the table, it is a circle in perspective, in other words, an ellipse (see Figure 3.9).

This study of a sphere can be done without the frame unless you are drawing the paper it is sitting on as well, as the shape of that will vary. (See Chapter 5, p. 63, Rectangles in perspective.)

(a) Start by drawing a circle, sketching round and round lightly with an HB pencil until you have several lines to choose from.

(b) Draw over what look to be the correct lines, as near the outside as possible, using short strokes only. Do not try to do it in one single line – only Giotto could do that to perfection! (The sketch lines actually help to make the circle more like a sphere. They add a slight shadow to the edge, making it look more solid.)

(c) To increase the effect of solidity, gently shade one side of the shape using soft curved lines of shading. Draw the arrow to show which side the light is coming from and make sure the opposite side is shaded. Start with the 2B pencil and change gradually to the HB as you get to half-way up, as this helps to make it look lighter.

(d) Add almost horizontal shading in the shape of an ellipse or oval to show the flat surface it is sitting on. You can only see part of the other side of the oval shape because it has the sphere sitting on it.

Complete the drawing with the background horizontal shading, making it lighter towards the bottom of the paper as before. Practise again with slightly less sketchy lines to start with. Each time the drawing will look better.

(Note that this can be demonstrated to a class on a white or black board, as children are quite familiar with converting white to black in other subjects.)

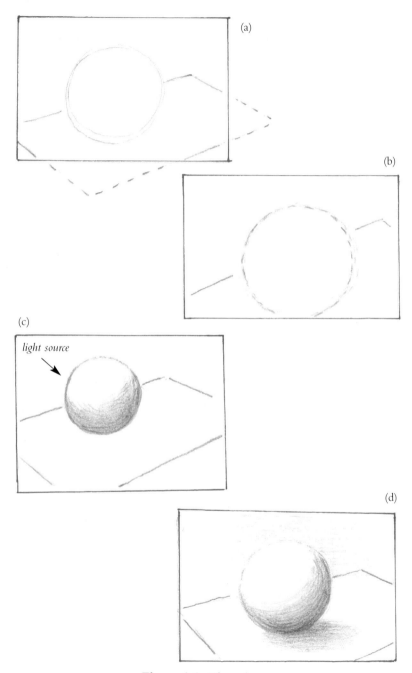

(a)

(b)

(c)

light source

(d)

Figure 3.9: The sphere

5 The rubbing-out method of drawing a sphere

There is another way to draw the sphere, which can look quite spectacular (see Figure 3.10).

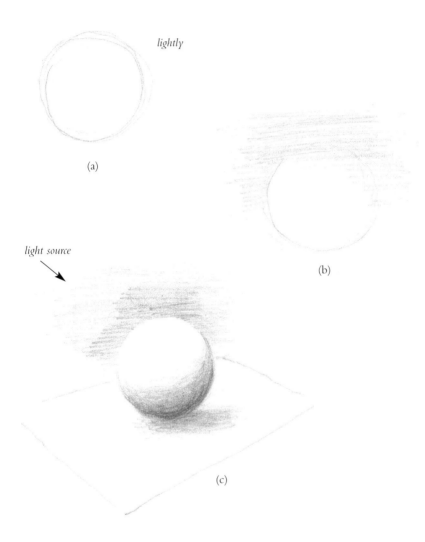

Figure 3.10: The rubbing-out method of drawing a sphere

(a) Draw the circle as before, very lightly. Decide which outside line looks best and rub out any other lines beyond it. Shade in the background, not worrying if it goes on to the sphere.
(b) Using a really good eraser, preferably one that has a sharp edge, rub out the curve *inside* to make the circle, and if possible some of the original sketch-lines as well. This leaves a beautiful white shape against the background.
(c) Shade in the dark side of the sphere with the curved shading, matching the curve to the shape of the top. All you need now is the elliptical shadow on the flat surface.

Follow the diagram slowly one step at a time until you are satisfied with the results, or start again until you are. If you find straight lines hard, make the drawing smaller. Short lines are always easier to do than long ones.

Note that the shading does not have to go to the edge of the paper. It only needs to be wide enough to show up the sphere clearly.

To keep the drawing fresh, a few extra lines are of no importance. If it is too perfect it will look like engineering drawing!

6 Simple perspective using the cube

When the cube is complete you can see the basic rules of perspective when you observe it carefully (see Figure 3.11). The same rules apply as when you studied the cylinder.

Move the frame up to study the top surface.

(a) From the corner, you can see that the shape isn't quite a diamond. The opposite sides are a fraction shorter than the near ones. This is because they are further away from you.
     (To demonstrate this easily, hold up your hand in front of your eyes. Can you see the room around it? It's difficult! Move your hand about 20 cms away. Now you can see round it because it is smaller. Even ten centimetres makes a difference to the apparent size.)
(b) Turn the cube so that the flat side is nearest to you. The shape has changed from a diamond to a perfect trapezium. This is because the further side, though still parallel to the near edge, looks shorter and both sides seem to slope inwards.

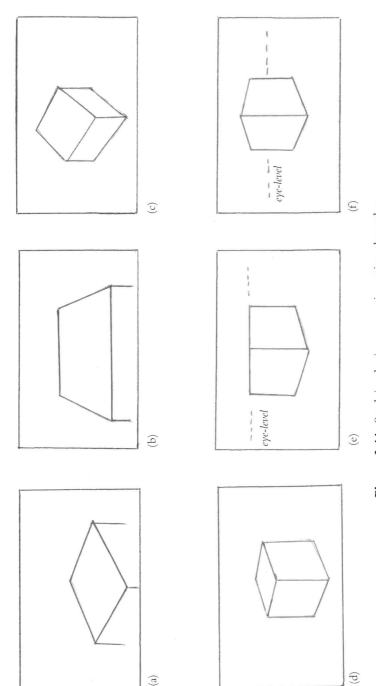

Figure 3.11: Studying basic perspective using the cube

This is a vital piece of observation. When you see and understand the fore-shortening, it will help you to draw all other shapes in perspective. It will also make it much easier to draw the piece of paper the finished cube is standing on.

The next diagrams show you what happens when you change your eye-level:

(c)   When you stand up, your eye-level – which is literally the level of your eyes if you look straight ahead – is much higher. You are looking down on the cube and the angle of the base, the V, is now very sharp. The top has become almost a square and the vertical sides now look like little parallelograms.

(d)   Move the eye-level below where it was for (a), and the 'diamond' becomes very flat and the V of the base is very wide.

(e)   Lower your head until your eyes are level with the top of the cube. The top is now a straight line, but the base, because it is still below your eye-level, is still a V, though a very shallow one.

(f)   Lift the cube vertically until the top is above your eye-level and the base is just below it. What has happened now? The top slopes down, but the base still slopes up slightly.

These are basic perspective rules:

•   All vertical edges stay vertical at all times unless an object is actually standing on a slope or is tipped up.
•   Any horizontal line below your eye-level slopes upwards.
•   Any horizontal line above your eye-level slopes downwards.
•   Any horizontal line on your eye-level stays horizontal.

See Chapter 8, p. 120, for more detailed information on perspective.

4 Working with the Children

Once you are feeling confident about these three basic shapes and the portrait, this is the time to put your toe into the water and try them out on the classes you teach.

If, however, you feel that you could do with more practice, then go on to Chapter 5 and come back to this chapter later.

1 Starting early

Having taught in secondary schools for many years and in primary schools for about ten years, I have had a chance to build on my ideas and have seen some amazing results. By encouraging awareness in their formative years, children can be enabled to absorb new concepts before their perception has been 'contaminated' by too much concrete thought.

It is not necessary to have a vast knowledge of drawing to help young children, but it is important to be able to draw some basic things fairly well, otherwise how can you expect the children to progress? However, improving their observation and awareness is an important starter.

Overcoming concrete thought

All small children start by having 'concrete thought'. For example, if one glass looks taller than another one does, then it is automatically 'bigger' and holds more than the shorter glass. Given two jars with the same number of marbles in each, one tall and the other short and fat, children will say that the tall one has more marbles in it because it is the 'biggest' one!

Children see all leaves as 'green', with no differentiation between the different shades of green. Sky is blue, even on a foggy day, and wood is brown. This is a pity, because there are so many shades and tones of the same colour.

Abstract thought

As we grow up, we gradually develop 'abstract thought', which means that we tend to refer to past experiences and to question and experiment using this knowledge. We begin to recognize similar known objects and to judge the possibilities and consider the probabilities when working out, for instance, which jar has a larger volume. We use our memories to associate with colours, shapes and sizes we have seen before.

In order to encourage children's progression to abstract thought, they need help in developing their visual memory banks. This can be achieved by exercises using the logical association of everyday objects, comparing sizes, colours and shapes, tones and textures.

Shape association

Playing observation games is a good way of helping to develop awareness in children of any age. A memory tray with several objects of a similar colour will test the children's ability to recognize shape rather than their colour memory. For example, you can use pieces of a child's toy tea-set of the same colour, or several of the same objects, e.g. four cups and only one saucer. Which is the odd one out?

When the children are drawing people's faces, introduce the egg as opposed to the ball. 'Which is more like the shape of your head?' Using two large card shapes and two small volunteers with very short hair, ask: 'Which is more the right shape for the head?' On the other side of the same card, have one pair of round eyes and one pair of oval eyes. 'Which look better?' You can also add, on the flipchart, two drawings, one with eyes near the top of the head, the other with eyes half-way down the face. 'Which look better?' They soon remember the egg and the oval eyes.

Years 1 and 2

Before the children start on, say, a picture of a house, it is worth asking 'What shape is it?' Is it like a box, with square corners but longer sides? 'What shape makes a roof?' A triangle? Well almost, but solid. They can look at a prism without having to learn the name. It is never too early to let them see the difference between a 2D and 3D shape. 'How many sides can you actually see?'

Trees never stop being like lollipops up until the age of about 10 if a child is never asked to look at the alternatives. Show them a ball on a stick and a natural sponge on the same stick. 'Which is more realistic? Why?' 'You can see through part of it.' 'Can you see the sky through parts of a tree?' 'Yes.'

When children are at the stage of learning to write, this is the best time to teach them to recognize a shape in known everyday objects – square shapes, straight shapes, round shapes, ∧∧ shapes, v shapes. Capitals can be likened to mountains, or the roof of a house, the wall, a bookshelf or whatever comes most easily to mind.

As children learn to write names, it is important to make sure they are beginning to recognize straight lines and curved lines. Ask, 'Is it straight?' and use a stick or ruler to prove it so. The mere fact that you are querying this will make them take another look. Use the vocabulary: square, straight, bent, curved, round and zigzag. It may seem somewhat insignificant at the time, but shape recognition is one of the basic skills of life.

Size association

To improve a child's ability to judge the relative sizes of objects, the simplest way is to start with a quick game of: 'What do we know that's as big as a . . . ?', 'What am I? I'm as big as a . . . but not as wide.' 'I'm bigger than . . . but not as tall.' Or you could try 'What do we know that is as tall as a door?', 'What would be small enough to go under the chair?' This idea of size association of familiar objects can be started very early on.

Colour association

Place several different coloured leaves on a tray. 'What colour are they? Are they the same green? What sort of green is this one?' A dirty green, a bright green, a dark and bluish green, a bright or yellowish green? This will not be as easy, but gradually the children can learn to associate with other known objects. Using several green examples, which of these is the colour of grass, and which is like the colour of a fir tree?

The shade of a colour is more easily recalled by association, as before, with known colours. Apart from 'sky-blue' you have: stormy-day sky, rainy-day sky, denim-trouser blue, sea-green, fir-tree green, grass-green, dirty post office van red, fire-orange, custard-yellow, mustard-yellow, muddy-brown, milk chocolate brown, plain chocolate brown, and so on, *ad infinitum*.

Texture association

What does hair feel like? Is everyone's hair the same? Liken it to known objects: Does it feel the same as carpet? Is it like cat's hair? Is it rougher than that? Texture is as important as colour and shape.

A 'feelie bag' is essential to a partially sighted child, but needs taking a stage further for others. What is more important is 'What do you think it *looks* like, does it *look* soft or hard. Does it *look* rough or smooth?' If they do not learn to look and not touch now, unless told to do so, it will become more difficult later. Otherwise they will continue automatically to touch things to judge the texture. When they are asked to look at an object in a science lesson, most children are still at the stage of touching things.

Tone association

This is the time to start to talk about tone as well as colour, for example: 'This is red, but what has happened to the other side?' (Light from the window shines on one side.) 'It's darker.' (A negative of a black-and-white photo shows this clearly but in reverse. It gives you the tones and stops you from looking just at the picture.)

If it is possible to demonstrate mixing two colours together, try mixing a little white with one colour: what has happened? More white, and what is happening now? It gets lighter and lighter. Then mixing black with it. What happens now? You get darker and darker *tones*.

You can also try, for example, red shapes on red paper or fabric. 'How do they show up?' Because the light shining on them is making shadows. 'Can we see a flat red shape on the same background?' Not really, because there is hardly any shadow.

Observation and awareness

The concept of visual awareness cannot be started too soon. It is essential to teach children to be observant, which in turn will improve aspects of safety in the home and on the roads and help to increase their concentration in the classroom.

At any age, games are always the easiest way to enhance awareness. I know that all teachers do this sometimes, but it is important to sharpen children's visual awareness in order to develop artistic and other skills. Keep them on their toes. Leave off a piece of jewellery after lunch, move your chair, change a picture or hold the pen in the other hand, then ask them: 'What is different this afternoon?'

You could move a vase of flowers, change the date, transpose the North and South labels on the wall, or change a shape on the maths display. Every room has something that the children usually ignore. If it is likely to change then they become more aware of it.

All these are 30-second additions that can be built on from nursery and reception level and will help to increase children's observational skills significantly.

Some children in a Year 3 class took twenty minutes to discover three things moved in their classroom because they hadn't had any recent practice. Year 2 took five minutes (during registration time) for the same exercise because it was done on a regular basis. They were far more observant and it showed in their work generally.

The skills the children will be learning will teach them a better awareness of changes in the classroom displays and the constant changes in their own environment, other than that it is a hot or cold day, or winter or summer. These days when VDUs and videos spoon-feed youngsters, they tend to leave it to others to make observations and comparisons for them.

Many children have a 'busy-book' at an early stage but by the third year most of them have a sketchbook, observation-book or art-book. Their drawing ability cannot improve very much unless they are taught to observe, and to translate that observation into a 2D representation on paper. Otherwise, bad habits continue and some children turn to comic characters or 'tags' because copying a drawing that is already on a piece of paper is easier than drawing from a 3D object. They 'close their shutters', as it were, and it becomes very difficult later on to persuade them to draw from real life.

Up until the 1950s, in many schools, children were told to draw carefully a small object in the room. This often consisted of a window-catch or the acorn on the end of the blind-cord. It helped to concentrate the mind, but these days there are many more interesting things in the classroom.

In all the time I have been teaching 'guided' drawing I have only had one comment, from a Year 3 child, that might worry some people. 'I can't draw. I can only copy.'

I was silent for a moment before replying. 'How did you learn to write then? Didn't you copy the teacher's writing and practise until you could do it on your own? We're just doing the same thing here aren't we? Just until you get more confident, then you can try drawing other things by yourself.'

You can demonstrate the way to place the shapes on the paper by drawing the paper and sketching in the shape. Children are used to copying diagrams and this is the same sort of thing. We are showing them how to translate a three-dimensional object into a two-dimensional representation on paper. They will become more and more confident, until they don't even wait to be told and will start drawing at home, bringing their work to school for your approval.

2 Points to check before any class teaching

Position

Check your position for drawing in the classroom. Sitting next to a flipchart it is difficult to see the angles that you have drawn. Straight in front is the best position, and the class also needs to see a drawing from as direct a line of vision as possible.

Draw a square on a piece of card and hold it up straight in front of your eyes. Now turn the paper slowly to 45 degrees in either direction. Watch how the shape changes to a thin parallelogram. The base and top lines now slope. Try the same with a circle and see how soon it becomes an ellipse.

The elongated angle is perfectly adequate for maths and language because numbers and letters can be read in an oblique form and understood, but with drawing the angle is more critical.

This is why it is so important to make sure that all the children in a class see a shape as square on as possible to start with and use a frame to observe the changes. If it is just drawn or seen in a two-dimensional form, many will make it whatever shape they believe it to be. The observant ones will make a good shape, but those not listening will make it tall and thin because that is what they see from their elongated angle and not what you showed them.

For demonstration purposes the children need to be within a 50-degree position of the centre of the board. They will then be able to go back to work, on their own, in their own part of the room.

Remember: you only have to be one step ahead of the class, not a brilliant artist. Whatever you do the pupils will think it is wonderful because it will be something they have never seen done before.

Using facilities to advantage

When demonstrating the various stages, a whiteboard is very difficult to draw on as any line that crosses over rubs out the previous line. This makes it impossible to do any proper shading or cross-hatching. The trusty old blackboard was ideal for this but a large piece of paper or card is a good substitute. (See Chapter 10, Figure 10.7.)

- A board pen is ideal for writing, but it is not good for drawing as it is impossible to vary the shade – it's black or black. It is also too wide for shading.

- Use instead a large thick pencil or a piece of pastel which can be held at an angle or on its side for shading, as the demonstration shape is much bigger than the A4 drawing that the class are doing.

- The lights in a classroom tend to cast diffused shadows. If the lights nearest the window are kept on and all the others turned off for a few moments the shadow will show more clearly. You might need a class decision as to where to put the shadow if there are windows on both sides of the room.

- Drawing is the one lesson where rubbing out is essential, so make sure that the erasers really do work. (We don't want ruined drawings on the first day!) Some seemingly lovely new erasers make the most awful mess of work done on a pristine piece of white paper.

Shape-drawing needs the rectangular frame to start with, and it is important to have it cut out carefully so that there are square corners, otherwise no one can see which edge of the object is straight and which is not. Some younger children may need help with this as well as being able to hold it level. It is also difficult for them to master the technique of moving the frame forwards and backwards to change the viewpoint and using only one eye.

If the lesson is about drawing the 10 cc cube, it is very important that, after talking about it and demonstrating it on the board, you place it on the group table so that every child has three sides in view (see Figure 4.1).

Cylinders and spheres need no such care in placing, as all the views are the same, but you need to make a point of stressing that the children should put the shadows where *they* see them and not where you showed them. A piece of A4 white paper placed beneath the shape shows up the shadows more clearly.

By the end of the lesson the quicker pupils could be drawing the rectangle of the paper. It will conform to one of the four shapes shown in the section 'Rectangles in perspective' (see Chapter 5, p. 63).

3 Introducing drawing to the class

This is applicable to any age group that has had no formal drawing lessons.

To encourage enthusiasm for drawing from the very beginning, it is important to give a big boost in the first lesson. All the class needs to know, as an introduction, is that drawing is nearly all looking and only a small amount of skill.

It is a good idea to start with the portrait. Practise it yourself a few times to boost your own confidence. The pupils need to see a reasonable adult drawing of a head and face, otherwise they will have no idea what they are supposed to aim for.

It is worthwhile starting with the children's own perception of the face, on spare paper, and then working through the portrait together with no special pencils or frame. The improvement will be dramatic and give the pupils a very positive attitude to the whole subject of drawing.

Introduce the frame, or the view-finder from Year 3 onwards,

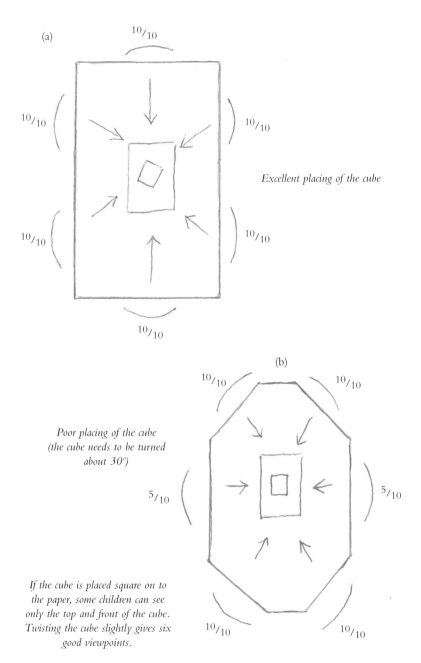

(a)

$^{10}/_{10}$

$^{10}/_{10}$

$^{10}/_{10}$

$^{10}/_{10}$

$^{10}/_{10}$

$^{10}/_{10}$

Excellent placing of the cube

(b)

$^{10}/_{10}$

$^{10}/_{10}$

$^{10}/_{10}$

$^{10}/_{10}$

$^{5}/_{10}$

$^{5}/_{10}$

Poor placing of the cube
(the cube needs to be turned
about 30°)

If the cube is placed square on to
the paper, some children can see
only the top and front of the cube.
Twisting the cube slightly gives six
good viewpoints.

Figure 4.1: All the children at the table need a $^{10}/_{10}$ view
of the cube

and work through the first three shapes sequentially, unless another topic makes one of the other drawings further on more appropriate. In this case, houses and trees may be needed, or perhaps some animals.

Achieving

When they have completed the portrait, the children will suddenly realize that there is more to this drawing than meets the eye! When twenty, instead of two or three, are good enough to display, they will look forward to their next session.

As we all know, achievement is the biggest incentive there is in making an interested and enthusiastic class. It is truly amazing what they can achieve once they have broken through the barriers of 'concrete thought'. There are no parameters laid down – each child must be encouraged to find its own. The boundaries are limitless.

All children need to believe in their own ability, to be able to pass judgement on others' work, beyond saying 'good' to everything. They have little or no concept of anything outside their world. Looking at a modern or abstract painting, surrealist or cubist, or looking at patterns and comparing them, evokes the response 'I like that one', not, as they should, 'that one is better because . . .'. They have no notion of good or bad drawing. All the drawings are better than theirs, so to them they are all <u>good</u>.

Give the children a chance to develop skills and when they can draw, albeit with a brush, chalk or pencil, then they begin to perceive the difference between the types of pattern or drawing. When they have had some experience with these tasks, the investigatory and exploratory experience will have given them a much broader base of skills from which to form opinions, a sense of colour awareness and the right approach to modern art throughout their lives. They finish up with a more balanced approach to life and an idea of which colours look best together, which coordinate and which clash or look gaudy.

Confidence

Confidence is based on experience, so with practice children will gain in confidence. We none of us know how far we can go. The more we practise the better we get.

Children need confidence to proceed. Starting with the nursery and reception classes we can build up their memory-banks and powers of observation and awareness. By the time they reach the top class of the infants' school they can draw a head, making it egg-shaped and remembering ovals for the eyes.

From Year 3 children can draw people of different age groups and simple figures in action. Their confidence is growing all the time. It is our job to take them as far as we possibly can.

Until your pupils have confidence in their own academic ability they are not able to present informed opinions. When they are struggling to produce good pencil-drawings or well-presented paintings it may confuse them to introduce, say, Picasso. How can they believe that good drawing is of value, when critics rave on about 'art' in the shape of a face with two eyes on one side, a calf in formalin or an unmade bed?

Constructive criticism

Constructive criticism is essential. Most teachers find themselves saying 'wonderful', 'brilliant' and 'well done' to a child to encourage them. 'Wonderful' means that there is no need for improvement, so they literally sit back and rest on their laurels and never strive to achieve greater heights.

With constructive help, the younger ones will see an improvement in their finished drawing. For instance, when they are drawing people, talking to them about their drawing also challenges their perception: 'Don't they look a bit thin? Could we make them look better if they had thicker arms? Would two lines look better than one?' 'Is her neck really that thin?' (No.) 'Can you add another line so that her head doesn't look as if it might drop off?'

The following points are useful to bear in mind when criticizing pupils' work:

- Try not to fall into the 'halo' syndrome. Look at your own and your pupils' work objectively. You know we can all do better with a bit more effort. Everyone can always improve, at whatever age.
- Children might need a little more input from you. Show them how to draw the shape on another piece of paper or encourage them to change one small part to improve the whole.

- Say to the children (instead of 'wonderful', 'fantastic', etc.): 'That's coming on really well', 'Is that really as short as that?', 'Perhaps, if it was a bit more rounded over there' or 'Could you try that again. Draw another one over there.'
- The first reaction is one of surprise and questioning, but when, with a little more effort, the whole thing has improved, they are delighted when you say 'O wow – that really does look so much better!'

4 Notes for class-work on portraits

Children may have some knowledge of the features of a portrait, but there is no harm in reminding them of the shape of the face and the relative proportions of the eyes, nose, mouth and ears. The easiest way to see what knowledge they have already is to ask them to do the 'before' drawing at the start of the session.

It is useful to 'test' their memory at a later stage especially before revisiting portraits.

With younger ones, demonstrating with the large circle and egg shape, as mentioned before, is often helpful as a reminder (see p. 46).

Work through the portrait in detail, as a question and answer session, gathered round the board, then go through it again as the children draw their own portraits at their tables. Later on some older classes may like to sit or lie on the floor to draw with you. It makes a pleasant change from didactic teaching and they enjoy working like students at art college.

By Year 3 the children can understand that the nose has no line down each side and reaches about 'half' the distance from the eyes to the chin. Year 4 can make a very competent drawing and even use some part of the character of their friends to personalize it. By Year 6, they should be able to cope with actual portraits of each other after the first full session. They can use the frame to check the shape and proportion of their friend's head.

Even in Years 5 and 6 it is important to remind them of their drawing in all relevant subjects, so that they do not think of it as a separate subject to be forgotten about in between drawing lessons.

Revisiting portraits

Visual aids

When pupils revisit portraits it is important that they see some examples of portraits from different centuries, from medieval times to the present day. Using only one artist gives them a very stilted and narrow view. Some early religious pictures, where drawing had not been developed, *have* got lines down both sides of the nose and eyes almost at the top of their heads. It will soon be obvious that the later portraits, which make the people look more natural, only have shading down one side of the nose, as well as eyes lower down on the face.

Using completely different examples of portraits, such as those by Leonardo da Vinci, and early pencil and pen portraits by Picasso and Lowry, proves that even 'modern' artists were excellent at academic drawing before they branched out along less conventional lines. Picasso's development from conventional to Cubist and Surrealist is particularly poignant. Portraits by Modigliani and Van Gogh show different ways of portraying the character of a person, for instance by exaggerating the length of the neck or the shape of the face, or adding brush-stroke texture.

Possible discussion ideas

It is vital that children understand how and why drawings and paintings were done from the Stone Age to the present day, not just what or who they painted. Were the artists leaving a record of what life was like or did they paint for a living? Are the subjects just rich people having their portraits painted, artists' models or family and friends? Did the artists paint someone just because they had an interesting face?

How many artists had time to paint self-portraits when to live they needed to paint what their patron wanted?

Leonardo was using ordinary people as models for commissioned big pictures, while Picasso and Lowry were drawing and painting their own families, and like Van Gogh were fascinated by the characters of the people around them. The subjects artists have painted reveal a lot about their reasons for painting them.

Were the artists being polite or flattering when drawing the person? Would they get paid if the portrait wasn't a good likeness? (For instance, if they made the ears look too big would the subject still want to buy it?) Artists did not paint very often for pleasure. To them it was work – hard work. If the customer was very rich, so much the better! A king or the Pope was the ideal person to work for.

Why did artists suddenly start making their paintings look so different? Why, for instance, did Van Gogh put texture on his faces? Artists were tired of making a perfect likeness, and when photography was invented, and became easier and cheaper, there was no point in competing. They wanted to make portraits different from photos. This was a rebellion against academic painting and a fairly new concept, worked on in a multitude of ways.

A trip to your local art college will show how varied art has become today. The artists there are young people struggling for recognition, just as 'modern artists' did during the last century.

5 Keeping a sketchbook

Working on pieces of loose paper is essential from time to time, but some of these inevitably get mislaid by the end of the year. In art we all need somewhere to keep those pieces. A proper folder, be it hand-made or reuseable, is essential.

Less well-finished pieces of drawing and sketching, which are just as valuable as a completed painting, need a home for safe keeping. Keeping a sketchbook is the only sensible way. Good expensive books are not readily available, but an ordinary plain paper exercise book is sufficient. It should be treated with respect as a dictionary of shapes for further reference.

The sketchbook can hold preceding work for a painting, or designs for 2D or 3D work. It is a valuable record of the child's development. Most importantly, it can be taken on visits or excursions and used to build up a bank of preferred shapes for any subject in the curriculum. Practising at home takes on a whole new meaning when there is a special book to put the work in.

From Year 3 or so, all drawings and designs can be kept safe for the entire school life, as a complete reference of work done, in a larger book.

5 Getting More Ambitious

1 Cubes and cuboids

There are many objects all around us that are made up of cuboid shapes: almost anything that has right angles, even with rounded corners, like a television. Part of some of these shapes are transparent, for example, between the legs of an upright chair, but we have to get used to relating objects to cubes, large and small. Look for the shape in a table, a sink, a cupboard, a cardboard box, a house, a computer, or indeed the room we are standing in. (See pp. 67 and 123.)

2 Different viewpoints

Different views of the same bookcase show that when we look straight at an object it is perfectly square, but if we walk to one side all the edges below our eye-level slope up, but the horizontal edge at our eye-level stays horizontal.

Anything taller than our eye-level, like buildings or even the television, has all the top edges sloping downwards away from us. If we were floating or hovering above the building, all the horizontal lines of it would slope upwards.

When looking down on a small plastic pyramid, the base shape is like the base of the cube, but if we stand near a real pyramid our eye-level is so low that the base looks almost flat.

3 Cylinders and cones

Many of the small objects that we have or use are a combination of cylinders and cones because the cylinder shape tapers at one end. (See Figure 5.1.) Pencils and bottles are examples of this.

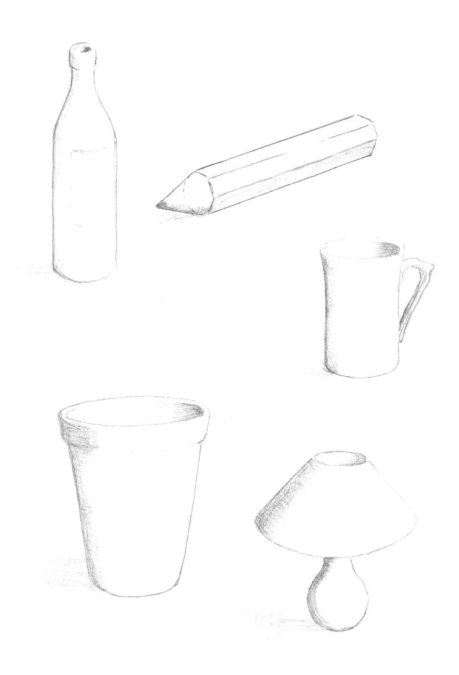

Figure 5.1: Cylinders and cones

Figure 5.2: Cylinders and ellipses

Look for the ellipse at the end of these shapes, if the circle is at an angle. (See Figure 5.2.) The top of the archway is also an ellipse. Wheels and round tables are all thin slices of cylinders. Look for the ellipse in the shape of bicycle and car wheels.

Most shapes in the world, including the human body are mathematical. They are made up of a combination of the three basic recognizable shapes (cuboids, cylinders or spheres). If you recognize the known mathematical shape and use the corresponding way of shading it, it will look really three-dimensional.

4 Rectangles in perspective

Rectangles from above

This is a shape that you can relate to the floor or wall of a room, the base shape of a table or any rectangle that is seen from the end, side or corner in any situation.

Take a piece of A4 paper and place it on the table. You know it is a rectangle but what shape does it really look like now? Remember the top of the cube and what shape that resembled? Is it a diamond? This is the same sort of shape, but it is elongated.

Use the frame to line up the end of the paper (see Figure 5.3).

(a)   Viewed from the short end it becomes a trapezium. Even in that short distance the far end has diminished considerably.

Keeping the frame horizontal at all times:

(b)   Move round the shape, corner by corner, in an anticlockwise direction. The shape you should see now is a long parallelogram, but the two sides away from you are shorter than the nearer ones. The parallel long sides would eventually meet at your eye-level to your right, while the two short sides would eventuall meet to your left. (The diagrams in Figure 5.3 have been slightly exaggerated to emphasize this.)

(c)   Viewed from the long side we have another wider, shorter trapezium.

(d)   From the last corner the shape is now the opposite of (b). The far end of the paper has now become the near end and is longer than the other end.

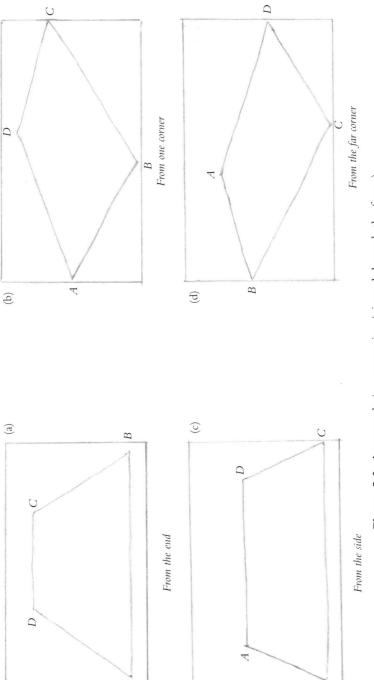

Figure 5.3: A rectangle in perspective (viewed through the frame)

Understanding this will help you to place correctly the legs of a table, the shape of a rug or mat from any angle. (If you are designing scenery for a play, this would make it easier to draw a room to look real for the stage.)

The rectangle from below
If you hold the A4 paper above your head you get the absolute reverse of the previous diagrams.

    These are the shapes to look for in the ceiling of a room, but of course, you never see the near corner or side that you are standing under if you are in the room. The ceiling diminishes as it recedes, just as the paper did. (See Figures 5.4 and 5.5.)

5 Studying the corner of a room

Using the frame
We know that in each corner of the room there are three right angles. (See Figure 5.4.) What shape do they look now?

    Stand to the left-hand side of the room.

(a) Look at the left-hand corner ahead of you. The wall ahead has a right angle and the vertical has stayed vertical, but the two other angles are much larger, forming open 'Y' shapes.

(b) The corner to your right is also a 'Y', the other way round, but because you are further away from it, the ceiling-line actually slopes down away from you and there are no right angles.

(c) Lower the frame to see the floor as well as the ceiling. The angles of floor and ceiling are in reverse.
    The nearer the wall you stand, the sharper the angles of the wall. This is like lowering your eye-level when looking at the side of the A4 paper.

(d) The right-hand corner viewed from the same place shows that the top of the window and ceiling lines slope down while the floor slopes up, at the same but reverse angle.

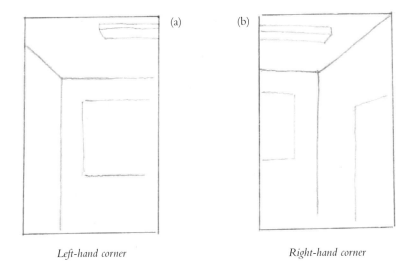

(a) (b)

Left-hand corner *Right-hand corner*

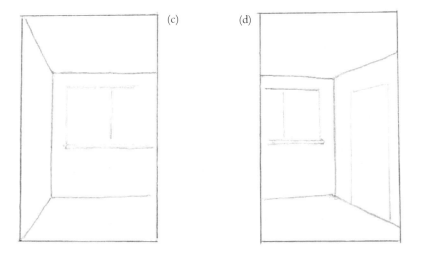

(c) (d)

Looking at floor and ceiling angles

Figure 5.4: Studying the corner of a room

6 Drawing an interior

Following on from the corner views, the two diagrams in Figure 5.5 show you the shape of the other end of a classroom.

(a) From the centre of the room, the far end is a rectangle because you are looking straight at it, not at an angle. The bookcase and oblong picture are all rectangles. Taking the top of the bookcase to be at eye-level, all the rectangular shapes diminish, walls, ceiling and floor. The door looks quite narrow from that angle.

(b) Take about three paces sideways to the right and all the angles change. The end wall now diminishes to your left.

The angles to your right are very sharp, while the angles to your left are less sharp. The base of the bookcase slopes upwards, but the top stays level. You can now see the end of the bookcase. The oblong picture, being above eye-level, slopes down. The door looks wider than before. You need to look very carefully to see these angles – in fact if you didn't know they were there you might not see them at all.

Try a sketch of a room, not a drawing just a sketch, as in the diagram.

7 Prisms

Prisms are found in house roofs, dormer windows, tents and Roman temples. There are many more that can be found – even in a chocolate bar!

You can see only two sides of the shape, unless it is held above the head. This shape is important because it helps when drawing the roofs of houses. Children need to see the prism when first drawing a house, but not necessarily to make a study of it.

The end is a triangle in perspective, with the point slightly over half-way across. (See Figure 5.6.) The base-lines form a V downwards, if you are above it, and a shallow V, upside down, from below. The far end, being further away, is smaller, so the roof looks thinner at the far end and the slope is a little shallower.

The same applies to the roof above the eye-level. Above your

(a)

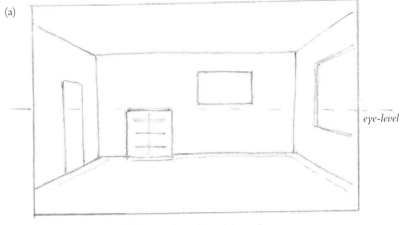

eye-level

'Square on' you have right angles

(b)

eye-level

From one side – no right angles

Figure 5.5: Drawing an interior

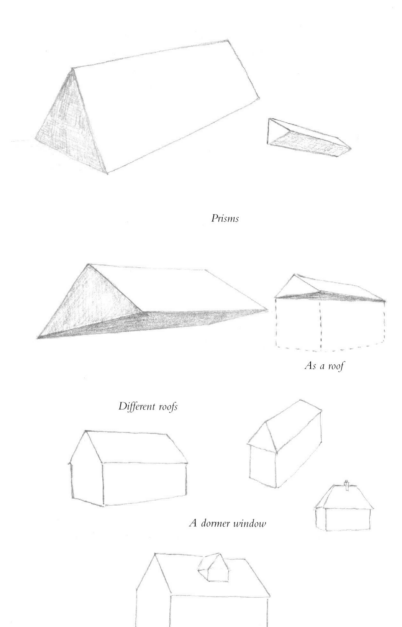

Prisms

As a roof

Different roofs

A dormer window

Figure 5.6: Prisms

head or below the two horizontal edges would meet somewhere on your eye-level, to the left or right, so the difference between the lines at the far end is only slight and many people can't see it until they are shown in a drawing on paper.

Houses tend to be at different angles to each other, not in straight lines, and the different slopes are not noticed, except by the careful observer.

8 Drawing houses

Houses are really just large cube shapes or boxes. Children are always trying to draw them, so this is a good place to look at perspective in relation to large shapes, after the study of the cube. (See Figure 5.7.)

(a) Draw the base-line: a shallow V with one side longer than the other. If it is drawn large on the board the children can look at it through their frames to see the angles. You could hold up a board ruler horizontally to help them.

(b) Three verticals need to be drawn from the V: the middle one is the longest, the one to the left the next longest and the right-hand one the smallest.

(c) Join the tops of the verticals. Like the prism or cube, held above eye-level, it is the same V in reverse. The far end must look the shortest.

(d) Draw the V of the end of the roof with the point a little more than half-way across the end wall, because the nearer half is always bigger.
From the tip of the V take the roof-line down, sloping a little more than the top of the wall, making the roof smaller at the far end.
Complete the far slope of the roof at a flatter angle than the near end (see the previous section, Prisms).

You now have a basic house shape. Figure 5.8 shows how to position windows and doors.

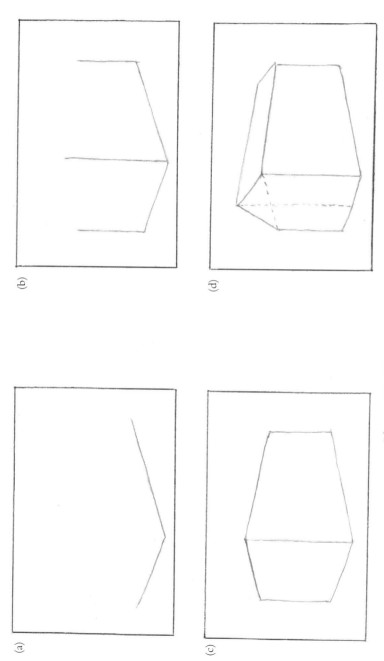

(a)

(b)

(c)

(d)

Figure 5.7: The house in four basic stages

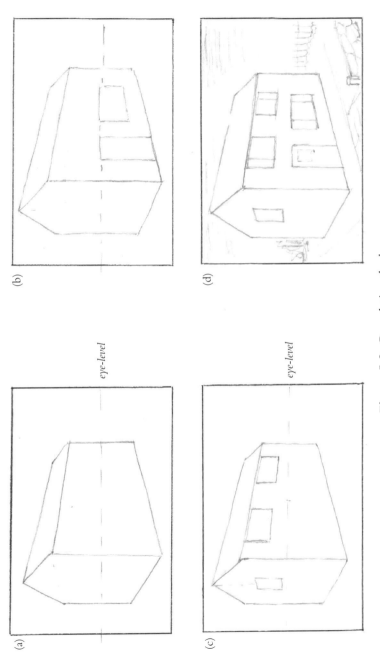

Figure 5.8: Completing the house

(a) Draw the eye-level across at about half-way up, as a dotted line to be erased later.
(b) Fit a door and a window below, keeping the vertical sides of each shape vertical at all times.
(c) Three-quarters of the way up put a sloping line in between the roof and eye-level. Fit some windows above that sloping line to almost touch the roof-line. (Most young children do not realize how near the top of the window is to the roof-line.)
(d) Complete the picture by rubbing out the sloping lines between windows and doors, also the eye-level line. Finally, add a garden with a path and some plants.

Windows

When we are drawing windows we must forget those 'baby' square shapes with a cross in the middle. (See Figure 5.9.) Look at any double-glazing advert. What a lot of different shapes there are to choose from!

Adding curtains does not necessarily enhance a drawing. They merely draw the eye from the main composition and, if not drawn well, are best left out.

Chimneys

A chimney-stack is just a cube on top of the roof but it does sit astride the roof which makes it harder to draw. See Figure 5.10 for the following stages in making an accurate drawing of a chimney:

(a) Rub out a part of the top slope. Draw the front of the tall cube, sloping both horizontals downwards.
(b) Draw the other edges of the top and third vertical down to touch the roof.
(c) Slope the near base corner up to the roof slope.
(d) The chimneys are just two cylinders above eye-level, so their top edges curve downwards.

Roofs

Roofs come in many shapes, but they are all prisms cut at different angles. The base is the same and the slopes are either long or short. The top always slopes at a steeper angle than the base

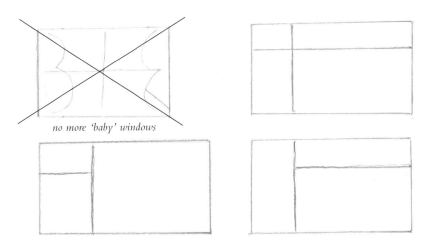

no more 'baby' windows

Figure 5.9: Windows

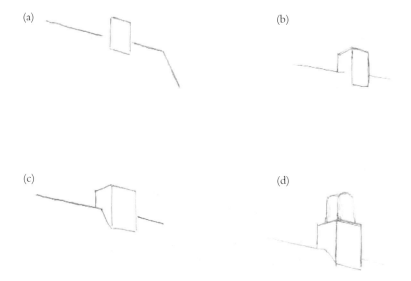

(a)

(b)

(c)

(d)

Figure 5.10: Chimneys

because the two lines would eventually meet at the horizon. The triangle at the end may be at any angle depending on the cut of the 'prism'.

Dormer windows are smaller versions of the same. They slope the opposite way to the roof slope. (See Prisms, p. 68.)

9 Shape-drawing in class

Having completed all the basic shapes, it is always advisable to have a practice from time to time. Shape-drawings can be used as a short class session. Up to three shapes can be given, and if the medium is changed to pastel, or chalk on dark paper, then it will not be thought of as repetition. Observation drawing will help the children and build your confidence as well. On dark paper both the shadow and the light side have to be shown, so pale and dark chalk are needed.

Groups of objects can be set up for class drawing. They could include a plant in a pot, a vase of flowers, a guitar, bottles, boxes and household items such as cups, mugs, kettles, etc.

Children do not have to draw all the shapes, but can choose those they are happiest with: curved shapes or flat ones.

It is important to remember that your own standing viewpoint is two feet above that of anyone sitting down, so some objects need to be nearer the floor to be viewed from above, otherwise everything is at eye-level or above, making it more difficult to get the right perspective.

When you have windows on both sides of the room, you may need to tell the children where you see the shadow and ask if they can see it. On a good day it is better without the lights on because the shadows will be darker.

6 Putting It All Together

1 Portraits of different generations

The QCA document for art (Years 3 and 4, unit 3A) contains a section that stipulates understanding 'relationships' or the difference between the generations. How better than being able to draw them! This is a very useful exercise when children have had some experience in drawing portraits.

The documents says: 'Use composition skills to make a double portrait that conveys ideas about their [the child's] relationship with another person in their lives'.

Unless they had already done some portrait work, children would probably draw two people of different sizes. But having worked on portraits before, children, using appropriate visual aids (i.e. portraits by artists through the ages), are able to understand about different facial proportions.

Examples of portraits of different generations include: Picasso's portraits of his son, also his portrait of his father from many years earlier; Dürer's self-portrait and *Head of a child*; Botticelli's *Birth of Venus*; and Rembrandt's self-portrait.

These pictures show people of different ages and demonstrate how the face changes as a person gets older.

We can make the following observations about changes in facial shape and proportions (see Figure 6.1):

(a) The young have faces that have not fully developed, while their cranium is almost adult size, so the eyes are below the half-way line down the face.

(b) Most women have a face that has eyes on the half-way line. This is not true in all cases but is the average proportion.

(c) In men the jaw develops more and makes the eyes appear

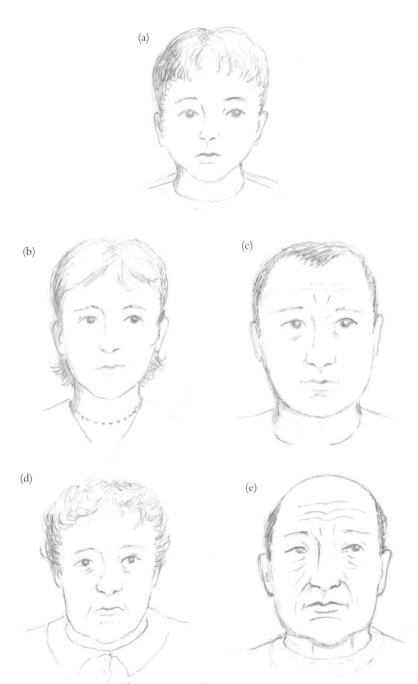

Figure 6.1: Different generations

slightly above half-way down the face. The sides of the head tend to be a little straighter than in women or children. Masculine necks are thicker and shoulders are much wider.

(d   As people age, their facial muscles relax and the flesh drops
and slightly below the jaw. This means that women's eyes now
e)   tend to appear above the half-way line. Men's eyes look even higher, which is accentuated when there is less hair on the head. In general, faces have more lines on them with progressing years and necks look shorter because the shoulders are more hunched.

- The eyes are about the same size in all the heads, but as the subject gets older the shape becomes less oval as the eyelid muscles tend to slacken.
- Drawing smaller heads means that the eyes have to be much smaller, so less detail is possible. However, the top eyelash-line is essential, as is the light reflection in the iris. The eye becomes an upward curve with an open circle of darker shading. The nose is softer with less shadow and the top lip shadow is more pronounced.

Note: Children have a wonderfully frank and honest way of portraying parents, bringing out the best and worst in their appearance or characters, e.g., 'My dad has a very fat neck and spotty chin'. And they are happy to show 'mum's lines on her face'. They reveal the basic character in a lovely simple way that adults would never dream of.

2 Three-quarter views of the head and face

When the head turns to the side, all the features are there, but slightly to one side. (See Figure 6.2.) This view shows clearly the shape of the jaw and the bend of the nose, which do not show from straight in front. The curve of the upper lip is more obvious, as is the shape of the lower lip.

When you are drawing a portrait at this angle, the subtle curves are possibly better seen through the frame. The more you look at the faces around you the easier it becomes to see the different

Figure 6.2: Three-quarter views

Figure 6.3: 'Luke'

shapes of jaws and noses. The only way to practise is to look at every face you see as a potential subject.

If you try to draw the same person twice they will usually look like someone else the second time. Sometimes the portrait will look better the first time, but sometimes the artist becomes more conscious of certain details the second time around. Look at the lack of detail in the small heads of Figure 6.2, compared with the far greater detail of the portrait in Figure 6.3.

3 Nature

To draw any living thing we need to understand its structure and observe it carefully.

Several curriculum subjects require drawings of trees, plants and animals. In science, the topics of living things, different environments, the food-chain, reproduction in plants and seasons are the first that spring to mind. In literacy, there are poems to illustrate. Trees, flowers and animals are often the subjects of poems, with all the colour and feelings that this involves. Observation comes into everything.

Trees in winter

A tree is made up of tubes that take water and minerals to all the branches and twigs, and 'food' from the leaves back to the rest of the tree by capillary action, like drinking straws, used upwards and downwards.

The base of the trunk has the combination of all these 'tubes'. They come from every tiny root and are all bunched together to start with. Each time a branch divides off to the side, the trunk is left that much thinner. It gets thinner all the way up, until there are only enough tubes for the smallest twig at the top of the tree. (See Figure 6.4.)

(a) In almost all trees the branches divide off alternately like the veins in a leaf. They never spread out at right angles, always upward and outwards, or the tubes couldn't take up the liquids, just as a drinking straw that has been bent, cannot be used to suck up the drink.

Looking straight at the tree you can see the branches to the sides, but remember that some branch off forwards and some to the back.

When you look at different types of trees you will see that each particular species has its own characteristics. The branches spread out, some turn downwards, some spread straight out, but the ends, in almost all cases, turn up towards the light to get as much sunlight as possible for photosynthesis to take place.

There are a few exceptions that do not turn up at the ends, mainly because the leaves seem to be far too heavy for the thickness of the twig. The palm tree and weeping willow are two of these.

(b) Using a soft pencil held at 30° to the page (sketching position), starting at the base, make an almost straight line up the page, working up and down to add extra thickness to the line towards the lower half.

(c) Return to the base and make it thicker and draw some alternated branches off to each side.

(d) Reinforce some of the bark by working over it several times and make the tree thicker at the base to allow for all the branches it will hold.

(e) Add more branches, in a slightly shaky way, to make them look more natural because there are very few straight branches in the world. Lift the ends and lift the pencil as well to make the line thinner towards the end.

(f) Divide the branch off into twigs and more twigs towards the outside edge of the tree. Work upwards and outwards, never inwards, as it is more difficult to make a line thicker than to make it thinner. I have never seen anyone do well when working inwards. (You would have to go back over the thickness of the branches and then over the trunk again and again.) To suggest the cylindrical shape of the trunk, add more shading to one side.

(g) Leave some gaps in the twigs as you add them. This will leave room for the leaves, or alternately suggest that there are more twigs than you have actually drawn.

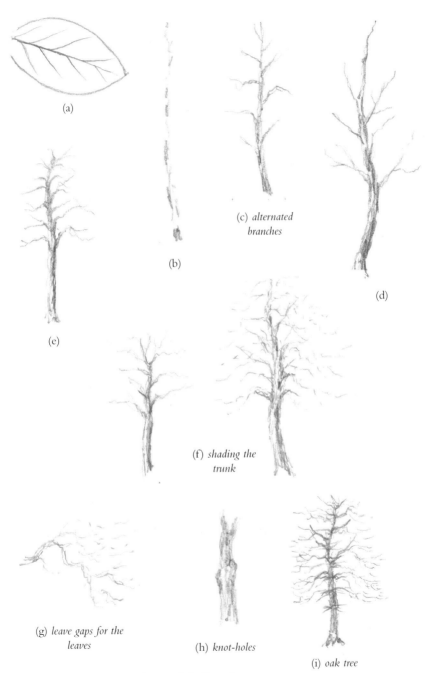

(a)

(b)

(c) *alternated branches*

(d)

(e)

(f) *shading the trunk*

(g) *leave gaps for the leaves*

(h) *knot-holes*

(i) *oak tree*

Figure 6.4: Drawing trees

(h) Add some darker, wider areas in the trunk to suggest knot holes in the lower third of the trunk.

(i) If you have added too many branches on both sides of the trunk as in this diagram, make some little spikes lower down and call it an oak tree!

Every tree, in every species, is different, like a person's face. A drawing of a tree will always look good, providing that you make the trunk look as if it equals the sum of all the branches and twigs. Also each branch must get thinner as each twig divides off.

Look at the trees in Figure 6.5. Each is a little individual with its own pattern of branches, but the way the branches spread out from the trunk is always typical of its own species. Each type of tree is a unique shape, some wide at the base, some tall and thin like the shape of a chilli pepper. To draw a tree in proportion, use the frame and look carefully at the shape around the tree to see the curves. Winter trees are like a skeleton of a leaf.

Some trees, such as the cherry (Figure 6.5a), have straighter branches than others and they divide into two several times. The silver birch (b) has branches that reach upward but the twigs 'droop'; however, they still turn up towards the light at the outer edge. Ash twigs (c) curl up dramatically at the end; the oak (d) has several branches dividing off at the same time. They are very twisted and each section of each branch seems to want to turn upwards. The twigs curl up at the ends and the trunk usually divides into two, near the top.

Trees in summer
Usually trees are much simpler to paint than to draw (the small brush or dry brush makes very good leaves), but to complete drawings of the tree we need to look at summer as well as winter trees. (See Figure 6.6.)

The leaves of the tree and the hairs on a human head have a lot in common where pencil-drawing is concerned. There are far too many to show all of them. This means that you have to suggest rather than draw each one. To draw a tree close up means drawing some leaves accurately. This is a tricky and painstaking task.

(a) *cherry*

(b) *silver birch*

(c) *Young ash*

(d) *Oak*

Figure 6.5: Trees in winter

(a) *Small cherry tree with leaves: close view*

(b) *Tall oak tree in the distance*

(c) *Cherry tree: closer view than (b)*

(d) *Large tree in the distance*

Figure 6.6: Trees in summer

(a) Complete the trunk in the same way as for the winter tree but make the twigs much paler as the leaves must look more important than the twigs.

(b) Leaves on large trees in the middle ground of a picture, not more than six centimetres tall, can have one-line leaves as shown.

(c) The cherry tree, being slightly nearer, has some two-line leaves. (See Figure 6.7(a).)

(d) In the distance the whole top of the tree, in leaf, can be suggested, as it is too small to put in all the intricate detail. The basic trunk construction can be lightly drawn, to show where the branches are, and the leaves suggested, in simple, curved lines, or little shapes, as shown.

Some parts of the branches should show between the leaves, but can look very false if they are not in the basic construction that was shown at the start.

Trees in pictures

Whether we are drawing something in front of us or drawing from our imagination, we can always employ what is known as 'artistic licence'. This means that you can move a tree to improve the picture, put it to the side, take it out altogether or relocate it into the distance to make a better composition. You are the boss – unlike, say, in maths, where the rules are laid down.

Leaves in smaller trees can become just lines (see Figure 6.7), but it is important that they are drawn at the same angle as the tree's own leaves. As you draw the lines upwards and outwards, lift the pencil off the paper at the same time. This makes the line thinner and is quite sufficient for a really good representation of trees in general.

(a) Part of a tree makes a very pretty border to a picture, as shown in Figure 6.7. Drawing part of the trunk up the edge of the paper and branches across the top on one side gives the picture a contrast between the near objects and those in the distance.

(b) Because the tree is a 'solid' it needs shading across the darker side, which makes it look more 3D. This shading on one side of the tree is especially good for showing one tree against another if there are two or more trees standing together.

(a) *A tree as a border*

(b) *Shading*

Figure 6.7: Trees in pictures

Compositions using the shapes

This is an ideal time to try a composition of a tree and a house, with curved hills in the background. If there is snow, then bear in mind that the shapes will be much softer.

Drawing a picture in pencil is an excellent way to understand tonal values before painting a scene. The right tones make a picture three-dimensional as it is essential to make one shape show up against another. It is easier to make the foreground darker at a later stage, but the distance is almost impossible to make lighter afterwards. Draw in the sky-line and lightly shade the hills, making the sky a little darker. In the middle ground, between the hills and the foreground, make the shadows fairly pale. In the foreground the shadows should be dark and the light sections left white for contrast.

Flowers

As with trees, we have to understand the structure of the plant to draw it. We are looking at a living thing, like a tree, that has capillaries running through it. Stems and leaves curve upwards and outwards when they leave the main stem; they cannot bend at right angles. Nature doesn't like straight lines; only man makes things absolutely straight with a ruler!

Most people start to draw without bothering to observe carefully. Look at the plant or flower and ask yourself these questions: Do all the leaves branch off together or do they alternate? Are the leaves straight or curved? Are there single leaves or leaflets, as in the rose? Are there three leaflets or are there five? How many petals are there, and how many can you actually see at any one time? (See Figure 6.8.)

Even in a science lesson, it is far more effective if you can draw a shape onto the board rather than give out a photocopy. Put the frame over the flower to see the exact size and proportion of the different parts. Practise a flower that you then find easier to draw, or study a new shape.

As with trees, all species are different. The dog-rose, the one used as a symbol for the Tudors, has five petals like many common flowers, including daffodils, violets and pansies, but the petal shape differs greatly. Others have more than five petals. Many house-

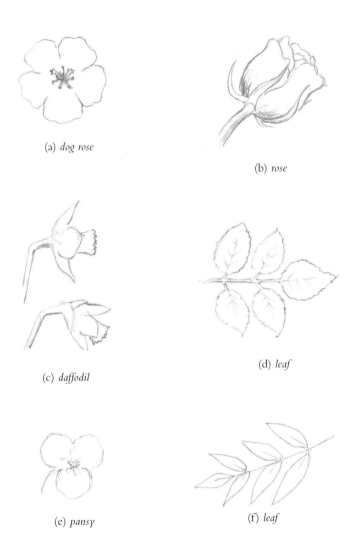

(a) *dog rose*

(b) *rose*

(c) *daffodil*

(d) *leaf*

(e) *pansy*

(f) *leaf*

Figure 6.8: Drawing flowers and leaves

plants and flowers are grown in distant parts of the world and are often different from what we think of as our native plants, and their structure can be complex and unusual.

Animals

At an early age, children often draw animals, for instance when illustrating a story or poem or when illustrating the food-chain in science, so Figure 6.9 gives some basic animal shapes.

As with all other drawing subjects, animals' bodies fall into shape categories: they are made up of circles, triangles, cube shapes, half-circles or ovals. Any animal can be just one mathematical shape or a combination of different shapes. Mice are ovals, while cats and rabbits seem to be a series of circles. Dog's heads look like rectangles from the side and their bodies are also elongated rectangles. Cows are very square and birds are mainly ovals. Observation is the name of the game as always! Look at the shapes through the frame to see which are which.

Horses are the most difficult to draw because the structure is complex and to do them justice you really need to study and understand the anatomy. However, some horse-lovers find them easy to draw, probably because they are familiar with the shapes and proportions.

Fish

Fish are lovely curved shapes that fit into elongated ovals. Some are long curved ovals and some short fat ovals that bend this way and that. (See Figure 6.10.) Ocean-dwelling fish are very streamlined and smooth in shape, but those that live in the coral reefs are triangular or square. Freshwater fish are a mixture of both. Each type has its own markings and has to be studied closely for an accurate drawing. Place the frame over the drawing and look at the curves compared with the straight edges of the frame. As with all studies of form and proportion, observation is the critical factor!

Figure 6.9: Animals

Figure 6.10: Fish

4 The human body

Drawing people is a very daunting subject for young and old alike, but becomes much easier when, like the portrait, it is taken in small steps. Thinking of mathematical shapes, the body is made up mainly of cylinders that are softened or flattened.

We start by drawing sections of a 'lay figure', the basic shapes only, making it easier to see the shape, size and proportion of each section. (See Figure 6.11.)

The head and face

When drawing the whole body, the facial features are much smaller and can be simplified to a few basic lines. When we draw

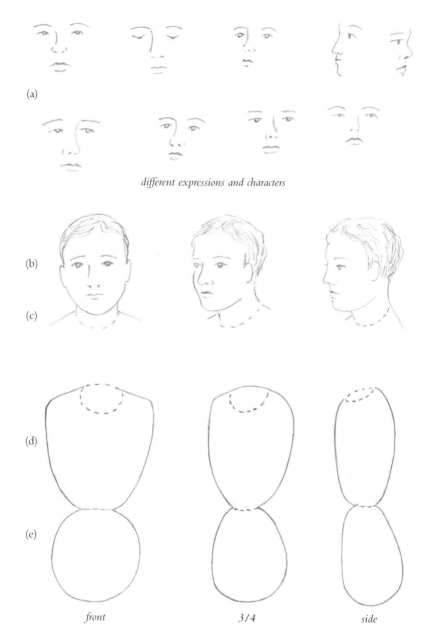

(a)

different expressions and characters

(b)

(c)

(d)

(e)

front   3/4   side

Figure 6.11: Drawing people: shapes and proportions

faces this small, the slightest change of line or curve can alter the expression and character of the face as illustrated in Figure 6.11a.

The head is, as you know, an egg-shape. It stays as an egg-shape from the side as well as from a three-quarter and side-view (b).

The neck
The neck stays as a cylinder from all directions, but as it sits on the front of the upper body (thorax), it appears to be longer from the side, as you can see more of it (c).

The upper trunk
The upper section of the trunk, the thorax, is a soft, solid D shape on its back, sometimes described as a beehive. The shoulders are about twice as wide as the head and appear from behind the neck. The length is about 1.25 times the length of the head (d).

The lower trunk
When you are drawing the lower body you will see that it is a softened sphere, looking circular from the front and pear-shaped from the side (e).

The limbs
The limbs are sets of differently sized cylinders that taper from the top down to the lower joint. (See Figure 6.12 (a), (b) and (c).)

(a) The upper parts of the arms and legs are more or less the same shape from the front or the side. They taper, or get narrower, towards the elbow and the knee.
(b) The lower arm is slightly wider just below the elbow, but tapers considerably towards the wrist.
(c) The thigh is much thicker than the arm, and tapers to the knee.
(d) The inside of the lower leg, the calf muscle, is pronounced, while the outside is a soft curve from top to bottom.
(e) From the side the same calf muscle shows strongly, but the front of the leg is curved inwards because the knee-cap protrudes. It is almost, but not quite, straight. A three-quarter view is half-way between the two.

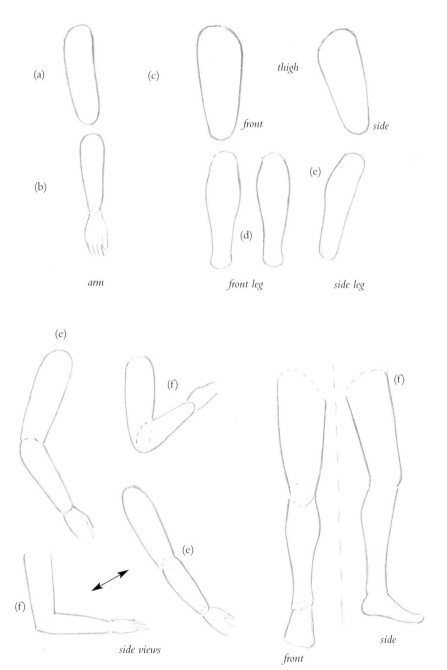

Figure 6.12: Drawing the limbs

(f) When you draw the whole limb together there is an overlap, as shown, to allow for the joint. The amount of overlap changes according to the position of the limbs. Where there is a greater bend, the overlap is greater.

Drawing the whole figure

In the male, the shoulders are slightly wider; while in the female, the hips are broader (see Figure 6.13). The two halves of the body are joined together differently for the male and female. In the male, the hip-circle is smaller and the two sections are separate.

In the female the two sections of the body are overlapping and the hip-section is larger than in the male. This makes the male hips narrow and accentuates the female waist. The skin between the two sections makes a natural curve, smooth for the male and rounded for the female.

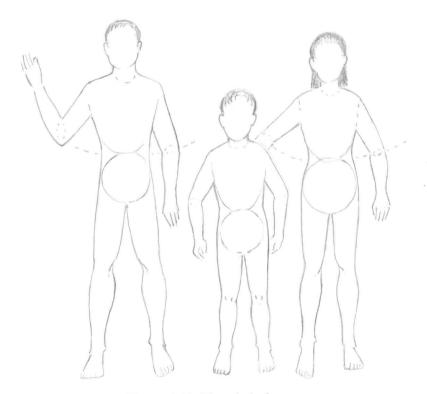

Figure 6.13: The whole figure

Proportions of the body

The adult male is approximately six to seven times the length of his head in height. Females are a little less. Children are from four to five times their head in height, according to their age.

To draw a male, start with the shape of the head and mark that length down the page six more times. Mark the paper three heads above the base and fit in the thorax and abdomen above it. Draw in two legs below that, the knee at about half distance and the triangle for the foot at the base of each.

The elbow is level with the waist, and the wrist, the bottom. Mark how far each should go and add them.

Hands are about the same length as the distance from the chin to the hairline.

This is a rough average for measuring out the body. If when you draw it it doesn't reach that far, then you can call it a younger person!

Side-views

We seldom get a true side-view because parts of the body usually twist to one side or the other. The copymaster section (Chapter 9, p. 132) has a side-view in it for gymnastic poses.

Hands

Hands have always been difficult to draw, and we can take heart that many of the great masters also found them difficult. (Figure 6.14 shows hands in different positions.)

(a) They fit into an oval when laying out flat, with fingers together.
(b) When open or holding something, especially from the side, they are very complicated to draw.
(c) Unless making a study of hands it is usually easier to 'suggest' hands rather than draw them. Often a soft oval with a suggestion of fingers will suffice.

Feet

Feet are slightly easier to draw than hands because the toes stay next to each other, but for detailed, close-up drawings they need to be studied carefully.

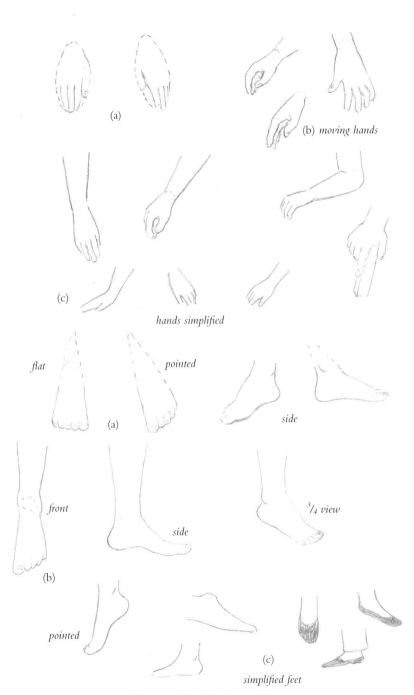

Figure 6.14: Hands and feet

(a)   Feet form a softened triangle from the front and from the side. (See Figure 6.14.)
(b)   From a top view the base of the triangle is at an angle.
(c)   Suggesting feet in a picture where the feet are small, the softened triangle is the simplest to draw and then a line across the toes to add shoes. Add an extra line below to make a heel. Only a study of shoes needs any real detail.

Bending the body

The body bends in the middle and the skin stretches or squashes between the two parts, as shown in the gymnastic movement below.

Figure 6.15: Gymnastic movements

5 Figures in action

Moving figures for Years 3 and 4

Children need to draw people in many different subjects. They are used to drawing stick men from the infants, but with help they can at this age learn the basics of 'people in action'. You might like to use Lowry's pictures to show them the 'secret' of easy people.

Lowry drew people in a very simple form. When people have jackets and coats on no real anatomy is needed. All you need to do is emphasize the fact that bodies bend and that arms and legs bend in the middle and nowhere else. Feet can be drawn like triangles and so can hands. Simple diagrams are all that is necessary. (See Figure 6.16 for some ideas.) There are a few to work from on the next page. If you start that way, in no time the children will be drawing lots and lots of people doing heaps of different things!

Children walking, pushing, playing, running, chasing, throwing, having secrets, feeling sad, talking to mum, talking to a supervisor, asking questions, and grown-ups helping or just having a chat — each curve tells a story. A slight bend of the body or even the head suggests a different mood. An arm up or down shows different feelings. A head down and with shoulders drooping suggests sadness.

Action drawing for Years 5–6

This part of the curriculum is usually for 10- and 11-year-olds, but if the children have already tried the Lowry people, they are perfectly capable of tackling this by Year 4.

Sportsmen and women have close fitting clothes on or vests and shorts. More of the body is revealed, so it is important to know a little basic anatomy.

First, the children need to revisit the proportions of the human body as a class, with some help from you. When they have a rough idea of the correct size and proportion of each section they should look at some sketches or pictures, from magazines or newspapers, of gymnastics and sports poses. They could collect a few from their favourite sport to see which parts of the body are hidden when a person is moving. The copymaster figures help to set out a pose for drawing. (See Chapter 9, pp. 131–2.)

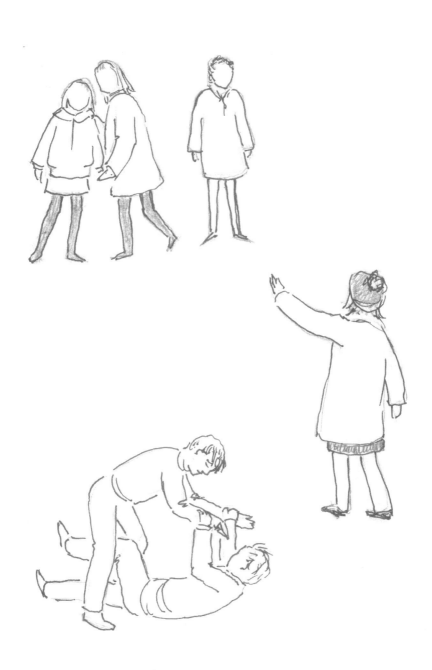

Figure 6.16: Action figures

It is important to emphasize here that action sketches and not careful drawings are the way to start. Begin with a stick-man in an action pose. Draw very lightly and then add thickness to each part. Do a sketch of a stick-man on the board or on paper, beforehand, and then fill him out as a class exercise.

(Drawing from a lay figure, or from each others' poses, means translating three dimensions into two on paper and is far more difficult.)

7 Working in Colour

1 Adding another dimension

Although not every art work has been preceded by a drawing in the form of a preliminary sketch, drawing is in effect the basis of many of the visual arts. Every painting is built up of lines preceding its later consolidation into coloured surfaces.

Only in the fourteenth century did drawing come to be recognized in its own right. Until that time it was merely used as the basic design for all two- and three-dimensional work. Most paintings are based on drawing, worked as a sketch beneath the paint or on a piece of paper, because paintings cannot just appear. They have to have shape and form. Mountains in the distance have form as do trees, be they in the foreground or away in the distance. A shape without form is a muddled scribble.

Children's dexterity in drawing is achieved by showing them how to look at shape and form and how to represent it in two dimensions. Those same skills enhance their painting ability. Not only that, but if we encourage them to experiment with colour, tone and texture, their pictures will have more form, depth and space and will be more three-dimensional. These experiences will help them to give informed opinions and truly appreciate work by artists past and present and to use their imagination to the full.

Most infants want to paint from the very first day in school, and probably before then. They are learning to control their bodies and the extension of them (i.e. the pencil and brush), learning the names of the primary colours and associating them with known objects around them. In school, they are also getting the chance to see and feel the texture of paint when making hand-prints or sponge and stick patterns. In class, they learn to draw with a brush and paint on a large piece of paper. Here they have a greater chance to practise than at any other time, because there are fewer subjects timetabled into the curriculum.

In order to help them to control the brush and use paint, it is essential to give some guidance with line, colour, tone and texture. In subsequent years, when time is more limited, they can then take full advantage of every opportunity. They can hone their skills and further experiment with colour to express emotions and paint from imagination to fuller effect.

Many adults have very little knowledge of how to mix even simple combinations of colour to make a different type of green or purple. Schools rarely teach these things and teachers are often as amazed as their pupils at the shades that can be produced with very little effort.

Working in colour is like opening a box of fireworks! The colours you can get are quite amazing. Every combination in the world can be made by mixing dark and light, bright and dull, no matter how subtle or strong.

Guidance

Left to their own devices, children will happily draw and paint at a very basic level, using any medium that comes to hand and all the colours available – Ten colours? No need to be choosy – just use the lot! School is there to teach them skills. Painting is an activity that requires dexterity like any other subject, especially drawing. It should therefore be a guided and to some extent a controlled activity.

Too often we rely on the children's own ability in painting to carry them through, and we may often be disappointed by the end results. We get used to a lower standard of work than is actually possible and turn to the one or two 'gifted' children to produce reasonable work to display. Once the pupils have learned to *look*, they can all improve beyond your wildest dreams. Having too much work to display is far better than struggling to find six pieces that *can* be displayed!

Teachers are missing the chance of taking their pupils several stages further on. It is quite simple to do, and I don't know why I missed the point for some years. It has given me so much more job-satisfaction, and it could do the same for you!

2 Different media and techniques

Adding colour to a piece of work can be done in many different ways. You can draw in pen or coloured pencil, use charcoal and pencil on the same piece of work or draw in pastels, chalk, water-colour pencils or paint.

Using one-colour washes

Draw the object or person with the pencil, but instead of shading, use a thin watercolour wash of blue or grey (a neutral colour) to show shadow and make the shape look more solid.

Draw with a pen and add the same wash. If the ink is not water-proof it will run into the wash in a subtle way that adds a 'third' colour and a nice smudgy effect. If it is waterproof ink it will just produce good soft shadows.

Water-colour pencils

Water colour pencils are designed so that when you apply plain water to the picture that you have drawn in them, it spreads the colours into the sections between. Use the pencil to highlight part of a painting and spread the pencil-line, using the water, if it looks too strong. This can be repeated as long as the paper is dry.

Oil pastels

Oil pastels are soft to draw with like other pastels, but like water-colour pencils when you add a wash – only this time of turpentine ('turps') or white spirit – the colour spreads like oil paint. Ordinary pastels are best on coloured papers, but these need a board or canvas to resist the oil.

Water-colours

Water-colours come in tubes as well as boxes. As the word implies, they are mixed with water to make them lighter, or very little water to keep the colour pure. Water-colour brushes are made of squirrel hair, sable or manmade fibres and are very soft, but come to points when wet. Good large brushes can be used for delicate work as well as broad areas. They are also suitable for the one-colour washes on drawings of ink or pencil. Any smudges can usually be dabbed off with a soft dry cloth or paper towel, unlike other media.

Wet-on-wet

This is a technique used in water-colour painting to add another dimension to a colour. It might, for instance, be used to show the different colour tones in the bricks of a house, or a sunset sky. It can be used on any shape in a picture – trees, hills or sky – but if repeated too often in one composition tends to lose its appeal.

- *Example: a house.* The work should be held at an angle on a board or easel. Mix the colour with a fair amount of water and start at the top. Mix a slightly different shade and continue in that, allowing it to spread into part of the first area. A third, slightly different, shade of wash could be added below as well. Each spreads into the one above, giving a subtle difference without a dividing line.
- *Example: a sunset.* Using only three colours (crimson, blue and lemon) the paper can be held upside down and worked from the yellow, to red, to the blue. It produces subtle shades from golden yellow to crimson, and from crimson to dark blue, making a spectacular sky through yellow, orange, scarlet, crimson to purple and blue. You can also get a lovely rainy sky by washing the whole area in watery blue and adding some crimson mixed with blue in the top area only as dark clouds. (See Chapter 9, Subjects from the curriculum, pp. 128–9)
- If the area to be painted is rather large this technique should only be done on thick paper, as it will crinkle and make gullies on thinner paper. (Sometimes these gullies can be used for a special effect. These are called 'happy accidents'.) If the paint dries too quickly the sky will have a rainbow effect.

Pen and ink

Fountain-pens are excellent for this as they control the flow of ink. Many cartoons and action figures work well in this media. (Biro leaves an uneven line and is less pleasing to the eye.) Pen and ink needs courage to begin with. There is no going back once started but pen-sketches are very effective. 'Happy accidents' is a phrase already used: what may not look good to you at the time could look very much better if you go back to it another day.

Oil paint

Oil paint is like poster-colour in some ways, but must be used on a primed board or canvas. The pigment is mixed with linseed oil, and many people find the smell unpleasant. There are few pupils under Year 8 who are able to use this medium successfully, and cleaning the pallet, brushes and fingers can be a messy business. The picture takes several days to dry and harden and is not really suitable for younger pupils. Brushes for this are round or flat and made of hog's hair.

Gouache

Gouache is pigment mixed with glue. Like water-colour it uses water as a medium and washes off even when dry. This is the same as school paint and needs a strong brush and thick paper. It is most suitable for large pieces of work, such as murals. Some 'water-colour' boxes actually have blocks of gouache instead of real water-colour paints. The colour is opaque and basic drawing can be done in charcoal which disappears under the paint. Used thinly, gouache covers pencil-lines and can be lightened by adding white. (Use oil colour brushes.)

Acrylic

Acrylic paint is rather like plastic emulsion paint for walls. It mixes with water but dries and becomes waterproof. It is thick like oil paint, but dries more quickly. It can be washed off clothes if it is still wet. (Use the same brushes as above.)

Charcoal

Charcoal is an alternative medium for pre-painting (i.e. drawing) material. Before they discovered the benefits of charcoal, artists working on murals drew with a metal rod. As a drawing material on its own charcoal is quite difficult to use because it is easily smudged and not so easily erased. Used with confidence and 'fixed' it is very effective as a soft drawing medium. It is used as the drawing material for gouache and poster-colour pictures because it disappears under the paint.

3 Perception of colour

When talking to children about colour, there is a very important point that we need to take into account concerning colour perception.

- How, for instance, can we be sure that what we call 'custard-yellow' is another person's perception of that colour?
- We have to query our own perception of colour because we cannot be sure that what we see in our minds is the colour the child sees in its 'memory-bank' of colour association. We may be thinking of the packet custard-powder yellow, while the child is thinking of that pale creamy mass that comes out of a tin.
- When we say red, which one do we mean? Do we mean the tomato-sauce colour or blood-red? When talking about colours, the class has to have a roughly uniform approach, and agree as to which of the shades of red, blue, green or yellow we are talking about.
- By showing the class three versions of any particular colour and asking which the children agree is the most like 'Post Office red' or blood-red, the green of the grass or fir-tree green, sky-blue or royal-blue, sandy-yellow or custard-yellow, hair-brown or wood-brown, we can quickly find out their 'average' colour perception.
- Talking about colours and comparing one with another is a vital part of a child's education. Oral and written descriptions will gain an extra dimension if they can describe colour with names that we can all understand.

Colour-blindness

A large proportion of males, young and old, are colour-blind, especially where varieties of blue are concerned. Some people are colour-blind, almost like canines, and cannot tell red from brown and green. All they can see are shades of grey and they have to differentiate by tone and use their memory. We need to be able to compromise for their sake and say 'the darker one' or the 'paler one'. It is important that children can tell the difference by the time they are old enough to cross the road alone by traffic lights!

4 Talking colours

A teacher needs to be able to talk about colours, and this is not necessarily a natural thing to do. Most children these days do not know the names of any but the basic colours, which seems a shame. Nor are they usually taught much about them. How can a child describe a scene accurately if all pale red colours are called 'pink'?

Building a colour vocabulary

Here is a simple example of how you might increase colour perception and description. Show the class five examples of pink that you can associate with weel known objects. The children then build up a memory-bank of names that they can all understand and relate to. For instance, you could have one very pale pink, two medium and two darker shades (baby-pink, peach, 'piggy-pink', shocking-pink and deep-rose pink). First show them all the colours, starting with the darkest:

- What colour have I got here? Pink? Are all the colours pink? Yes they are.
- What sort of pink is this? Dark? Very dark or fairly dark? Fairly? Have you ever seen anything this colour? Not sure? What about a rose? Yes.
- What about this second one? Very bright? If you can't think of a name for it, what about the pink on a Valentine card? It's called shocking-pink.
- Now how would you describe the third one? Is it baby-pink, or is it too dark for a baby? Too dark? What about 'piggy-pink'?
- Is this a baby-pink? No, it's too yellowy. Have you ever seen anything that colour? Not sure? What about a peach? Well that is what it's called: peach.
- Now we come to the palest colour. What would you call that? I said it before didn't I? Yes it's called baby-pink.
- Now let's see if you can remember all those names again!

Later, if you show them a reproduction of a famous painting, the class can try to describe some of the colours the artist has used. They have to build up a vocabulary of colour names in order to help their descriptive work, whether oral or written. When they are able to use 'deep blue' and 'velvety' to describe the night, instead of just 'dark', then we know that we are getting somewhere.

Reinforcing colour-recognition
The ability to describe colours cannot be taught like the ABC. It comes from experience in making those colours. Talk about colours that the pupils have mixed, especially if there is a 'new' colour not seen in class before. They should be able to say how they came by the colour, and that helps to give it a name. Is it a more 'bluey' shade of green or a yellowy shade? What does it make you think of? Grass-green looks different at different times of year. It can look misty or 'bluey' in winter, yellowy in spring, bright in summer and more 'browny' in autumn. Colours can look smooth or rough, velvety or like satin.

What does the colour make you think of? How best can you describe it? Try giving the colours names that the pupils can associate with school or something around it – even someone's hair-ribbon or sock colour. My favourite was 'faded fisherman's jersey', which nowadays is probably more like faded jeans colour.

I once listened to a Year 6 class struggling to describe the scene outside the window. It made me determined to improve children's vocabulary of size, shape and colour. I hope you will find 'talking colours' useful.

5 Using the imagination
Young children find imagining very difficult because imagination is based on observation and experience. Heightened awareness and observation should soon be achieved in their drawing sessions but they are never too young to experiment with colour, if encouraged to do so.

Give them as many experiences as possible by changing the colours they can use and showing them how colours are used to show feelings and moods. They will remember the different colours better if they have mixed them themselves.

Investigation

Investigation is the name of the game. Problem-solving and the skill of mixing colours can be started in the infant school. This is a process which needs to be taught as children cannot usually do it by themselves at this stage. By the age of 9 they should be able to mix colours automatically, without having to be reminded to do so.

Given a limited number of colours to mix, some of the pictures might seem to be a little 'individualistic', in that they might look strange, but the children are learning a very valuable lesson. Remember that there is no absolute right and wrong with painting. It is the way they see it, from a different perspective or perhaps a different height! The colours they use might look strange to you, but then some children may be slightly colour-blind or just lacking in colour-association experience.

One point to bear in mind is that if you use a similar coloured background to the colours you have given them, the whole thing will have 'harmony'. It also means that they do not have to cover the whole page with paint, just the middle section. Like drawing, a large piece of paper, especially if it is white, is very daunting.

If you guide your pupils through the first stages, the end results will be so much more pleasing. You might need much more display area for the excellent results, but this is hardly a downside to their work!

6 Experimenting with limited colour

Three colours

This first stage of exploration is simple. The children are to paint a picture. All you need to do is to slightly 'complicate' the task by limiting the colours available at any one time. The one colour that should be left out is green because it is not a primary colour and the most natural green is the one that you can mix.

Crimson, blue and lemon-yellow are the best colours to start with because the only colour that cannot be replaced properly is black. Black on its own is a negative or dead colour and all pictures look much warmer without it! Use it only to darken other colours later.

Leave it to the children to do the investigating and experimenting. The most exciting colours can be displayed for all to see.

Give the children a piece of practice paper and ask them to mix the colours that are missing. Which colours are missing?

- Green? Well, how do we make it?
- Orange? How do you make orange?
- Purple? Which two colours do you think make purple?
- White? Well, we can use that if we need a much lighter colour.
- Black? Use the darkest colour you can mix instead of black.
- How do you make a good pale skin colour? Many skins are mainly brown and white, but what about the palest skin? (How many non-painters know that the secret is to add a touch of green to make the pink look slightly translucent?)

Crimson, blue and lemon yellow can be used for almost any painting you could possibly mention. White paper gives the lightest parts and you have a combination of shades through yellow to orange and red. The blue gives you pale to dark blues, depending on the amount of water added, and greens from the palest to turquoise, from pale mauve to dark purple. Add a little yellow to the purple and you get a brownish colour that is not as deep, but far more effective and warm than any black.

As the children develop, you will find that they enjoy the challenge of limited colour and rise to the occasion in every way. In the end, the skills that they learn (which are vital to their over-all development) will help them to describe colour far more vividly.

Colour combinations working with three colours

As with learning to draw, when starting to work with three colours it is better to start with simple mixtures and work up to the more complicated ones. Use the primary colours – red (crimson), royal blue, lemon-yellow, black and white – before going on to the 'chemical' colours. (Scarlet is crimson with added yellow but could be used as an alternative to crimson as it helps to make a good brown when black is added.)

There are so many combinations to choose from, so here are a few of them:

- Crimson, blue and yellow: all the colours you need for many pictures that include purple, but there is a better brown with less mixing if you use scarlet.
- Scarlet, yellow and black: these colours make excellent autumn pictures, sunsets, especially over water, with silhouette mountains and trees, and silhouettes suitable for deserts with palm trees. Also try Bethlehem and the star, the Great Fire of London, Guy Fawkes Night and bonfires.
- Yellow and back and white: these colours will yield a wide variety of shades between yellow and subtle greens. There are at least twelve versions of black and some may have a bluish tinge, so you might get some slightly blue greens into the bargain!
- Crimson, black and white: start with white and make a colour that only just shows up on white paper. Add crimson in tiny drops to make a total of six or seven different shades. Black adds lots of grey shades of the above.
- Blue, black and white: work in the same way as above.
- Crimson, blue and white: as above.
- Red, yellow and white: as above.
- Blue, yellow and black: as above.

You might also like to give the children a colour-scheme exercise, such as: 'Paint your mum in blue, black and white! How does she look? Happy or sad?' This is the beginning of mood painting: see also the section Monochrome below (p. 114).

Chemical colours

These colours include turquoise, viridian green, purple and orange. Used singly with white, they are very suitable for imaginary paintings on imaginary themes – dreams, moods, planets – and painting inspired by music (e.g. Holst's *Planet Suite*, Handel's *Royal Fireworks*, etc.).

Note that by adding black and white the number of colours is more than doubled.

Opposite colours of the spectrum

Purple and orange and red and green are opposite colours of the spectrum. These make a composition that is very effective, and adding white adds extra tones to the picture. The colours are 'complementary' and work well when blended together. Used without mixing they clash.

7 Two colours

When they have explored painting in three colours, try giving your pupils just two. Blue and yellow are a good choice for experimenting with mixing. Give the children a subject to paint that needs green or two shades of blue: for instance, a house and garden, a tree with a swing, spring-time, sunshine on sand and sea, etc.

'Concrete thought' says, 'Sea is blue – sky is blue. Trees are green – grass is green. How can you paint them together on one piece of paper when there is only blue or yellow paint?' However, younger children have no notion of 'too difficult' and will tackle any subject given. Help them *never* to adopt a negative attitude, or they will lose their confidence.

Tone and texture in painting

When painting, the tones of the colours have to vary to show up against each other. A pale object always shows up better against a darker colour or tone. Making a lighter tone means adding more water or white to the first colour; to make a darker tone add a darker colour (preferably not black as it will deaden the colour). In water-colours it is better to use less water to get the richer and darker tones.

The colour of grass in the foreground of a picture has to be darker than the colour in the distance, otherwise there will be no sense of distance in the painting. The same goes for any shade of a colour – even the sky looks paler towards the horizon. This does not show up very clearly in a photograph and is not always easy to see with the naked eye, except perhaps when looking at distant mountains. It is a logical point that has to be remembered when trying to paint space and distance.

Texture can easily be added when the paint is thick by making some of the paint so thick that it stands up off the paper. Below is a simple lesson, suitable for children of Years 3–4 on making pictures with only two colours and adding texture for effect.

Exercise in two colours with texture (Years 3–4)
You need the following materials for this exercise:

- white A3 paper
- blue and yellow poster-paint only (a dash of scarlet is optional)
- a little PVA glue
- a small sponge
- three brushes

Using just two colours, blue and yellow, mixed with a little PVA glue, pictures of grass, cornfields and hedges, etc. can be achieved.

- Without PVA, paint the blue sky in the top third of the paper in any way – with or without clouds. Let it dry a little.
- Next, using the yellow that has PVA glue in it, paint the cornfield in a big strip below the sky and use a sponge to add a speckled effect on the sky edge at the top of it. Make it thick and sticky for the best effect.
- Take a stick or end of the paintbrush and scratch vertical lines in the yellow, to make it look like the stalks of the corn.
- Using the glue, mix a pale green, starting with yellow and a dash of blue, and paint some grassy strokes across, below the corn, in a stripe and scratch in the grass.
- Add more blue to the green to make a sticky, much darker green and finish the bottom stripe of the picture with more grassy strokes (vertically). Again, with the pointed end of the brush, scratch taller grass, radiating outwards in tufts, along this green. If it goes up into the paler green, so much the better.
- The pointed end of the brush could also be used to add a few scarlet spots on the yellow to look like Monet's poppy fields!

8 Monochrome

This stage of exploration is quite complicated as the pupils have to understand how to make a colour lighter by adding water. They also need to be able to recognize tonal values, or shading and shadows, because this is where we use a wash and pen or pencil. (It would look bizarre if they painted a whole picture in blue or green of the same depth!)

One colour pictures in water-colour can look like sepia photographs. There are endless possibilities for experimenting with this technique. Add water, and it looks paler. By drawing some shapes in wax before painting you can get paler marks in some places making different textures. Using poster-colour, if you keep it thick, you can scrape through it with a point to make lines in it. The pen or pencil shows through light washes, which gives yet another tone.

Whole pictures can be drawn or painted in monochrome. Snow scenes showing footprints and shadows, snowmen and snowballs can be drawn in blue crayon, wax crayon or painted. Solid blue can be used for the tree, side of a house or any dark object. These monochrome pictures are also very effective done in browns. (See, for instance, Monet's snow and stormy-sea pictures.)

The most important point is that the children learn to use dark against light, to make one object show up against another, or different tones or textures rather than different colours. When they have mastered this concept they are able to cope with monochromes of any colour: orange, green or whatever.

Painting in one colour
How many teachers, especially in the primary sector, have had experience in mixing subtle shades of colour to express emotions, thoughts or feelings? To express anger in seven shades of red is far more realistic than in red, blue, green, yellow, black and white. (A summer's day in those same colours would be meaningless! That would be far more effective in five or six shades of yellow.) Pictures can be made using only one basic colour. Monet did this with his sea and snow pictures.

This exercise is suitable for all children in Year 6 who have had colour-mixing experience. Each pupil should have an A4 piece of practice paper. Then proceed as follows:

• Mark the paper off into twelve squares.
• Using poster or water-colour the children then have to mix twelve different blues.
• Start with white and add a tiny drop of blue (it should not be much darker than the paper).

- Paint the first square on the paper.
- Add a little more blue and fill in the second square (the only stipulation is that it looks different from the first).
- Work up to one square of the neat blue.
- The rest of the shades are made by adding any other colour to the mixture.

You might well ask: How do I know if it is still a blue? In order to find out, ask yourself the following questions: Is it a red? Is it a green? Is it a yellow? Is it white or black? If the answer is no to all these, then it must be a blue.

Blues include sea-green, through turquoise to mauve and a blue-purple, from white to almost a black. There are more tones of blue than just twelve but with twelve, there are enough for almost any picture.

Seas and mountains are obvious choices for 'blue pictures'. (See Pablo Picasso's Blue period for some ideas, but almost any subject can be painted in any colour that you care to mix.)

One-colour blue pictures are useful for 'sad', 'lonely' or 'cool' subjects, also for pictures with an imaginary theme, such as 'The Blue Planet' or 'A Sad Dream'.

Green pictures suggest countryside and fresh air. Yellows suggest hazy days of summer, the heat of the desert or dry grass-land in Africa. Reds could be hot and angry pictures, and with lots of purple and violet suggest magic, witchcraft and mystery.

Few primary schoolchildren at present can produce mood pictures because they have had neither the opportunity to investigate colours nor the practice in mixing them. We must try to give them the skills and the chance to achieve beyond their present ability.

Some of the resources you might like to use for one-colour pictures are as follows: Modigliani's portraits; Picasso's Blue period; Turner's misty landscapes; Monet's bridges in all seasons, as well as his sea and snow scenes, or his orange picture of sunset over water. (And of course you can always fall back on photographs of planets.)

We hope that in time this work will form part of the junior curriculum, enabling secondary pupils to undertake more complex adult tasks.

9 Dexterity with the brush

If you go on giving children large brushes and pots of sticky paint when they are beyond Year 2, it is as good as saying, 'We don't expect you to paint well – so splash about a bit, and here's an apron so that you don't get it on your tummy!' This is not giving them a real chance to improve their skills. But you do need to help them through the frustration of not getting it absolutely right, which we all suffer from (if we are honest).

Why should children wait to see if they are good enough to go to art college before they are taught to draw and paint! The world is full of frustrated artists, and we are here to help them, and to enable people from all walks of life to find out that painting is a wonderfully relaxing and fulfilling pastime (and frustrating, if we are honest!).

Because painting is relaxing for so many people who have had no training, why is it left as a sort of placebo in school? Just think how many more excellent artists we might finish up with when we show them more about it while they are still children! That would help to take the elitism out of art, and perhaps people everywhere could learn another way of relaxing, instead of freezing at the mention of the word and saying, 'Oh, I'm no good at painting', or ' I can't draw at all!'

By the age of 7 children love having a brush that goes to a point and paints that they can control. They are tired of 'messy' painting and prefer something they can do and keep clean. Children don't always like a messy task. There have to be the same rules of course: limit the colours and mix to make the colours that you need, or the nearest you can make. (And no cheating!)

Water-colours

There are several types of water-colour boxes. The ones with the round shaped colours are less like genuine water-colours than the ones with the rectangular-shaped paints. The basis for water-colour is the drawing, and those lines show through the colour, so it is easier to paint the shape and the detail is still there through it. Poster-colour, or gouache, is so thick that the detail is lost when you paint over the lines.

Note: The first time that children start painting with water-colour brushes they feel as if they are using a pencil and tend to hold the brush at a low angle. This smudges the edges. They need to be reminded to rest the hand on the table and to hold the brush almost vertically. They can also turn the paper upside down to paint the opposite side of the section, which they may not have tried before.

10 Water-colours: a whole-class activity

For this exercise you need the three colours: crimson, blue and lemon.

When using water-colours you need to remember that they look much paler dry than they do when wet. This is because the paper shows through the colour. The palest colour will be any pale colour with mainly water, and the darkest colour will be the three colours mixed together with very little water. This dark colour is rich and velvety and replaces black, which, as we have seen, is a dead colour when used undiluted.

By mixing these three basic colours, you can get some amazingly bright and subtle shades and whole-picture harmony.

The following exercise works very well with a whole class of children above the age of 7 or so, when they have had some guided lessons and done a good drawing on cartridge paper as a base for their painting. (If they have never used water-colours before, it might be a good idea to photocopy the original and let them practise on that first. There is always a back-up then if anything goes wrong, especially with Year 3.)

- For every two pupils, you need: one water-colour box, one waterpot, a large and small water-colour brush each, a mixing tray (if the pallet is rather small) and some paper towel. (The table should stay perfectly clean because this sort of painting is neat and careful, and should be done accordingly.)
- Take the large brush and using water swirl the *hairs* of the brush only round in the paint to gather up some colour. Use the ridged edge of the pallet to squeeze the paint into the bowl of it. Rinse the brush swiftly and do the same in the

next colour. Now gently mix the two colours together. (This is to emphasize the fact that squirrel-hair brushes are very soft and break if the metal part of the brush is used for mixing.)

- Get the children to hold the brush more like a pencil and rest their hand on the table, to be more accurate with any edges.
- Instead of trying to paint to the line on both sides, from one position, show them how to turn the paper round to make it easier. Everyone has one side that they can paint easily, usually the side that is furthest away from the pencil or brush hand.
- As the surface covered by a brushstroke is smaller than that of the poster brush, the best sort of subject to start with is something that fits the middle of the page, and not right up to the edges (e.g. an Egyptian artefact, a person in Victorian costume, a portrait or a character such as a Roman soldier.)
- Using water-colours is the one time that painting wet-on-wet is really effective (see Chapter 7, Different Media and Techniques, p. 105).

Children can learn to mix all sorts of subtle colours, and the results will amaze you and your colleagues. Let them try mixing some colours on practice paper before working on the picture itself.

8 Going Further

1 Do we really understand what we are looking at?

Most people will say yes to the above question but in fact they don't truly understand what they are *seeing*! Their brains tell them what to expect, therefore they don't look in detail at what is before them. The short cut to understanding is *observation*. Proper observation means a *new* understanding. Believing what you are looking at is not enough. Analyse with careful observation any object and use your newfound skills to convert the solid three dimensions into a 2D shape, not necessarily to draw at that moment, but note the angles and how you could put them down on paper.

Be aware that the viewer, that's you, must be looking at the object in a direct line, straight in front, to see the true shape of it. If the viewer or the object changes in any way, to the left or right, a square ceases to be a square and becomes thinner. The circle ceases to be a circle and becomes an ellipse. In your head the brain is still saying 'circle' while your eyes are noticing the change. Let your eyes tell the brain what it is looking for and with careful observation you will then see it as it really is.

Eye-level

Eye-level is the level of your eyes wherever you are: sitting, standing or even flying.

(a) Up on a mountain you can see further, but all horizontal edges converge towards your eye-level. If your eye-level is higher then everything vanishes to that level (see Figure 8.1a).

(b) Here you can see that anything at your eye-level stays at your eye-level. All the people in the street have their heads at

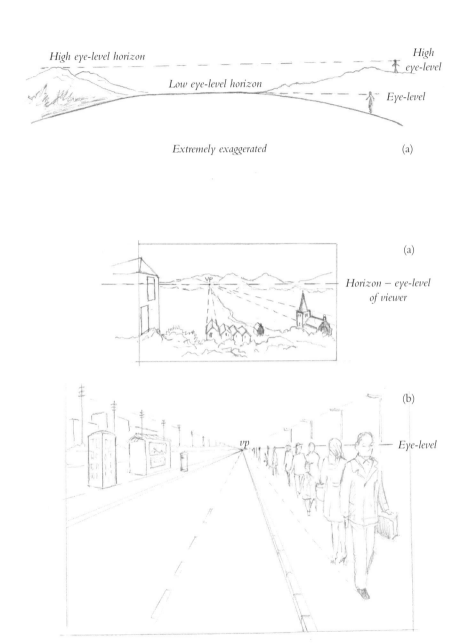

High eye-level horizon

High eye-level

Low eye-level horizon

Eye-level

Extremely exaggerated

(a)

(a)

Horizon – eye-level of viewer

(b)

vp

Eye-level

Figure 8.1: Eye-level

about your eye-level, but appear to get smaller when they are further away. All the shapes further away converge towards your eye-level.

If we could look at the world as if through the frame we would be able to see the slightest changes as they happened. The frame held correctly gives us the horizontal and vertical, the benchmark from which to judge angles.

2 The vanishing-point

The vanishing-point (vp) is the point at which parallel lines appear to converge in the distance, usually on the horizon, when there no hills in the way, or to a point in space where they disappear or cease to exist. On a flat plane this is at eye-level.

Imagine you are standing at a level-crossing. Look at the rails straight in front of you through the frame. They are parallel. Turn your head slowly to the right and see how the tracks slope up into the distance getting closer and closer together until they merge and disappear. The same happens to the left. Those are the vanishing-points. This must not be confused with the horizon because if the tracks were uplifted vertically there would still be a vanishing-point up there.

The vanishing point is still there even when it is obscured by a hill. In a room, if all the furniture is square on to the walls, all the horizontals will meet straight in front of you at eye-level. If a stool (a) is at 45° then it has different vanishing points to either side of the viewer.

If everything is at 45°, as in the buildings shown in Figure 8.3, there is a vanishing-point on each side, out of your line of vision. This diagram shows the vanishing-point on each side and the rectangle shows you the part you can see without moving your head (i.e. your view).

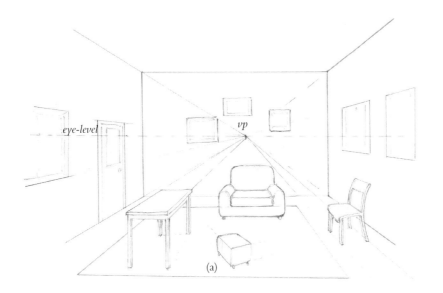

Figure 8.2: Vanishing-point obscured

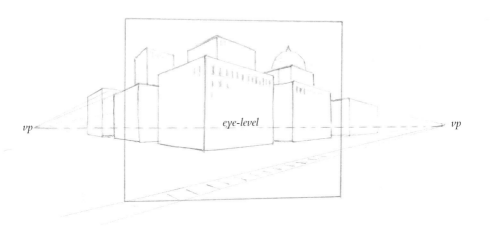

Figure 8.3: A 45° angle

3 Perspective

We dealt briefly with perspective in Chapter 2. Here is a brief recap on the basic rules of perspective:

1. Verticals are always vertical, no matter where the horizontals are. Whether uphill, down a slope, near or far away, they are always vertical.
2. Horizontal lines are only horizontal if they are at your eye-level. Above eye-level the 'horizontals' slope downwards towards your eye-level. Below, they slope upwards to your eye-level. They all converge towards eye-level.
3. All horizontal parallel lines meet eventually on your eye-level at the horizon. They still meet at eye-level even if you can't see the horizon, for instance, in a room or if there are hills or slopes in front of you.
4. The only time that parallel lines are parallel is when you are looking straight at them. Step to one side and look at the same two parallel lines. Then point 3 applies.

Trying out perspective with a ruler

The foreshortening of perspective can be worked out using a ruler, but one should never try to keep ruled lines in the drawing as it loses all 'life' and becomes too mechanical. Use very light pencil for the construction lines and draw the verticals freehand because a ruler covers part of the picture and obscures the lines. Try to finish the whole drawing without the ruler.

The paper should be landscape to allow for the vanishing-point. Draw a dotted line across the paper about halfway up the paper, about 11 cms (see Figure 8.4). On this line make a cross on the left-hand side. This is the vanishing-point for all the horizontal lines.

On the right, mark 6 cms from the top, point (a) and 8 cms from the bottom of the page, point (b). Join these two marks to the vanishing-point, keeping them pale to avoid distracting from the later drawing lines.

Draw a darker vertical line (c, d) freehand to make the first corner of the house. Add another vertical further across to complete the front of the building.

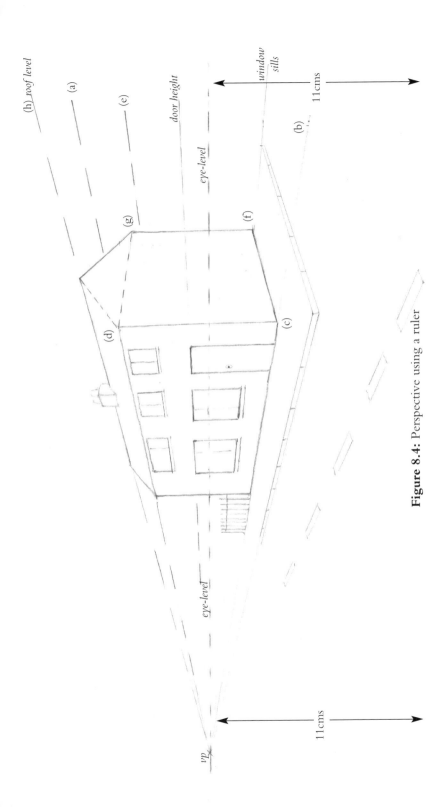

Figure 8.4: Perspective using a ruler

Everything on the front of the house diminishes towards the vanishing-point, e.g. tops of doors and windowsills, but verticals must remain vertical at all times.

The eye-line is below the top of the door and downstairs windows, so add door height and window sill lines a little above and below it. Put in some vertical lines for the door and downstairs window.

From the vanishing-point take a line across halfway between the door height and the top wall line (e) and another line for the top of the windows as shown. Draw some more verticals for the sides of the upstairs windows and darken the horizontal sections of the door and windows.

For the side of the house draw sloping lines (c, f) and (d, g) and draw (f, g) vertically between them. The roof line (h) is not far above the top of the house because we are looking up at it. Make a V from the roof line down to the verticals halfway across the side wall. The only part left is the far end of the roof which is a shallower slope than the near end, from the roof line to the top of the wall.

Freehand darken all the lines of the house that are still very pale, but if you wish to add the chimney leave the roof line until that is finished. (See Figure 5.10, p. 73.)

To start the roof, all you need is another line a little above the top line (h). Make a V down to the verticals starting a little over half-way towards the rear wall. The only part of the other end of the roof showing is a slope a little shallower than the one at the near end. Add a chimney as in Figure 5.10 (p. 73).

Once you know and understand what you are drawing, all you need is practice. Later on you can try to draw a line of two or more small houses, in perspective, without any ruled lines!

Look carefully at the picture and see how even the line in the middle of the road converges towards the vanishing-point. The fence verticals get closer and closer together and the kerb-stones soon become too small to bother with.

9 Ideas and Projects

1 Subjects from the curriculum

We all need resources to work from and, unlike other subjects, in drawing we can 'shop around' for material. We cannot put together a picture and make it look natural unless the details are realistic. Using the books and pictures from history, geography, science or literature gives us material to last a lifetime. We should never be short of ideas.

We need to show our pupils that drawing and painting is *cross-curricular* and not a separate entity. It should never be 'pigeon-holed' into being one period a week and then forgotten. Use at least one idea from each of the other subjects per year. This should still give you plenty of time to finish design, technology, pattern and 3D work or observational drawing. There are enough subjects below to keep you and them busy for the next ten years!

Costume, people, houses, trees and vehicle pictures

Give the class lots of drawn, painted or photographic examples, even photocopies, and suggest, as well as show them in very rough sketches, how to assemble a composition. Draw two rectangles in 'landscape', and say, 'Put the houses here at the back, on this or that side, and if you find the cart/carriage difficult to draw, put it behind the people. Who could be at the front, here, or here?' You need only draw rough shapes to show where you mean. It gives them alternative ways of setting out the page to the best advantage, and the rest is up to them. It is a far greater help than just saying 'Draw a Tudor street', or 'Paint a picture of people in the rainforest'.

Illustrations and diagrams for science
Most pupils need help with drawing things like aeroplanes and/or cars, people and hands for topics such as forces. Your guidance is especially important when they are working on the topics of space, habitats or environment. They will need basic help with animals, plants and trees in order to raise the general standard of their illustrations.

Literacy illustrations
Literacy lessons generally cover a vast range of subjects that are ideal for art classes. Children may like to illustrate poems or stories they have written or read. There are so many paintable subjects: the weather and the seasons, storms, winter rain, washing blowing in the wind, sunsets and silhouettes, the seaside in a storm or on a hot day, misty days, foggy days, dreams, scenery for a play they have written, and many more possibilities.

History illustrations
History offers all sorts of subjects for drawing and painting: Egyptian pyramids, temple paintings and boats, round houses, and Roman or Tudor houses. Pupils could try a Tudor or Victorian portrait, or even a family portrait showing the different generations. There are memorable scenes from different centuries, for instance, the Great Fire of London, the beheading of Charles I, or Guy Fawkes preparing to blow up the Houses of Parliament. Costume also offers endless possibilities: drawings of clothes, hats and hairstyles, royal regalia, suits of armour, uniforms and fashion from different centuries.

Geography illustrations
Geography topics include drawings of jungles and rainforests, deserts, polar scenes, mountains and volcanoes, valleys and waterfalls, and different trees: cedars, palms, redwoods, etc. Any environment and its people that the children are studying at the time can be used as a subject in their art classes.

Music and drama
Here we have the opportunity for drawings and paintings that show moods and feelings, possibly on a chosen subject or after

listening to a piece of music. They can involve happy or sad, lively or peaceful emotions. It would be appropriate here to experiment with one-colour work (see Chapter 7, p. 115).

RE
The different religious festivals – Christmas, Easter, Ede, the Festival of Lights (Diwali) – that children learn about or take part in all make good subjects for illustration. So too do places of worship: churches, mosques, temples and synagogues. This work can be done in addition to the various shapes and patterns (e.g. religioius icons) associated with different faiths which can also be drawn or painted in the art lesson.

PE and games
Sport offers a huge variety of action poses and pictures. Magazines, newspapers and photos are all good sources for pictures of footballers, tennis-players, athletes and gymnasts. (See Figure 16.6a, p. 100.)

2 Practical resources
The frame
Before the first class session on shape, copy and photocopy the quadruple rectangular frames onto A4 paper. Give yourself some spare copies for mistakes. It is not much use giving children card frames as they lose them easily – even with their names on them.

*   Show them how to pierce or snip the centre with the scissors without damaging the edge (not folding the paper), and cut out to one corner along one of the curved lines and make the edges as smooth and straight as possible (see Figure 9.1). Remember to add the 'portrait' and 'landscape'.

The copymaster figures
The paper cut-outs (Figures 9.2 and 9.3) are of a front and side view of the figure. Photocopied larger, onto A4 thin card and joined with small paper fasteners, the figures can be put into any number of poses to show children how the body moves.

The copymaster figures bend rather too well to be really

 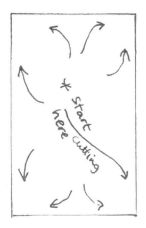

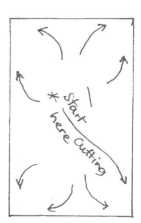 

Figure 9.1: Copymaster frames

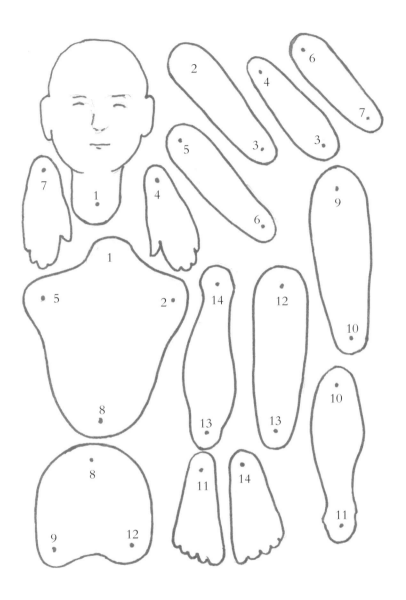

Figure 9.2: Copymaster figure (front view)

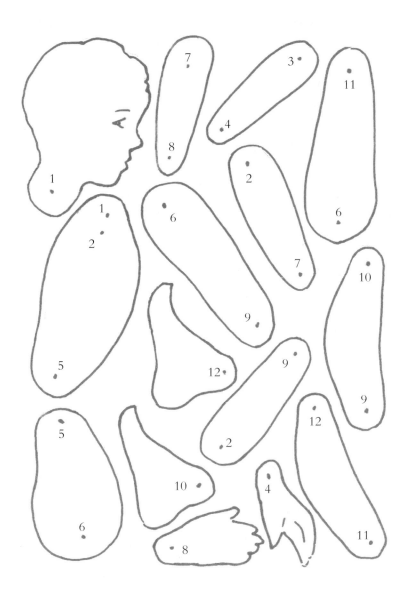

Figure 9.3: Copymaster figure (side view)

human, but, when laid down on the table, can be arranged into all sorts of athletic and gymnastic postures ideal for sketching.

A group of children could work on a mural depicting a spectacular scene, or sequence of movements, by drawing round the figures and then adding vests and shorts, socks and gym shoes, completing it in any media, paint, pastel or chalk. Adding some background floor colour is essential, or the figures look as if they are floating. Given thicker clothes and pale blue shadows from their feet, the figures will look as if they are skating, especially if a few blue lines stretch out behind them.

Figures with clothes can be attached to a window in a sequence to make up such moves as a forward roll or cartwheel. From the outside it becomes a series of silhouettes.

3 Teacher resources

Some teachers, especially those in inner-city schools, often fail to realize that the children they teach seldom explore deep into the country. Many of them are whisked off on foreign holidays and never get to investigate their homegrown flora and fauna. Their lives are often dominated by videos and TV programmes which fail to clearly distinguish between the real and the make-believe. Children need to experience things first-hand to understand the world around them, especially things like the Life Cycle or Food Chain.

Give them real resources, and not just in the infants. Borrow an animal for an hour (preferably with its owner?). Have real resources in the room. Collect some wildflowers, different grasses, feathers, tree bark, a branch of a bush with its leaves still on it, etc., things indigenous to this country and let the children look and touch, feel the texture, and compare size and weight. During any spare moment they can always draw them. Learning from experience is vital for their visual memories. It helps their observation and awareness and will increase their drawing and illustrative skills.

4 Communications resources

Internet and CDs

As an alternative to borrowing books from the library, use CDs and the internet to build up your own and the children's resources about famous artists past and present. *The Encyclopaedia Britannica* has illustrations of a wide range of paintings, portraits, abstracts, pottery past and present and sculpture which you can show the children. They may like to do this research for themselves.

Websites
Use your LEA website and contact other schools in order to share ideas and display your children's work. If the pictures you need are in someone else's book, they can be scanned for use in your own classroom.

Libraries
Your local library will exhibit work done by the children not only in 'Book Week' but all the year round, using pictures taken from all areas of the curriculum. It costs nothing, but you may have to book the space beforehand. This is an excellent way of showing the children that they have achieved work of a high standard.

5 Competitions

Once your pupils have made great strides with their work, they will be keen to show it off. Competitions are a good way to do this. Many organizations – businesses, charities, banks and building societies – regularly hold competitions to design posters, advertise products, etc., and will happily send details on request.

Competitions are often advertised through your LEA, so it is worthwhile checking with them to see what might be an appropriate outlet for your children's work.

6 Excursions

Art colleges
Local art colleges usually hold exhibitions of students' work at least once a year and this is an ideal opportunity to show the children what they might achieve in a few years time. However, this sort of visit is best kept for those children who have had experience with different media and who are able to understand most of the techniques involved.

Galleries

Trips to art galleries, as we all know, take a lot of organizing. Transport to them can be very costly, so it is essential that the children you take will be able to get the maximum benefit – otherwise it will be rather a waste of time and effort! If you are thinking of a trip to an art gallery, it is worth considering the following points:

- Try to find an exhibition that is relevant to the work the children are doing at that time, rather than an all-purpose 'educational visit'. Galleries are full to bursting with work of all sorts and it is too much for younger children to take in or appreciate. Be selective.
- Children's own development to some extent reflects the history of art. Let them see the types of paintings they can easily relate to. Those still at the 'primitive stage' cannot really appreciate academic work, but would love cave paintings and Lowry people! A child that has made excellent progress and whose work corresponds to, say, the early Renaissance period will enjoy the Italian school of painters, and will be able to appreciate the attempts at perspective, colour and shape in them.
- What is it saying to 7-year-olds if you show them Surrealist pictures while they are still learning to draw? They can empathize far better with, say, Van Gogh and impressionist painters, because their work is more natural, and that is what they themselves are trying to achieve.

Pupils need to understand that 'modern' artists were academically trained in the first place and that Surrealism and Cubism, or whatever, were a later development in their art, not a starting-point. Maybe it was done out of frustration or boredom with the commonplace! Picasso's development through photographic to simplified and then to Surrealism and Cubism was a rebellion against society and was meant to shock the public. Instead of shocking, however, it was eventually acclaimed and became the in thing to do!

Every great painter has made an important contribution to the world, so there has to be a chance for young minds to experience as much as possible – but not all in the same day!

10 Examples of Children's Work

Examples of children's work are a vital part of this book because it is important that all teachers everywhere see how much their pupils can achieve in a very short time. The examples given are taken over a period of eighteen months.

Not many people have given Years 2–3 the credit they deserve. They have always been able to 'draw' to a certain extent, but few teachers ever seem to push them forward or give them a goal to work for in drawing. They can look, see and draw, and are amazingly perceptive! Given the chance, by Year 3 they show real promise. These first-session portraits in Figure 10.1 are just a few of the 25 examples the teacher had that were so good she had to put them all up! In the corner of each you can see the 'before' drawing to compare with the finished product.

The tree and house studies (Figures 10.2, 3 and 4) by children of the same age are remarkably well observed and competently drawn. Later on, these same children were able to tackle 'different generations' (Figure 10.6) and subjects from Chapter 9 (see Figure 10.7). It is wonderful to see a habitually disruptive boy in Year 3 working hard on his drawing with amazing results, or a statemented child join in wholeheartedly and do her first real drawings in Year 5!

Years 4, 5 and 6 had to start at the same level as the Year 3 children as regards technique, but their advanced manipulative skills enabled them to make better progress once they had learned to observe carefully (see Figure 10.8) and to advance to good shape drawing (see Figure 10.9). Figures 10.10 onwards show examples of their cross-curricular work (see Chapter 9) with relationships and historical portraits.

Figure 10.1: Portraits by Year 3

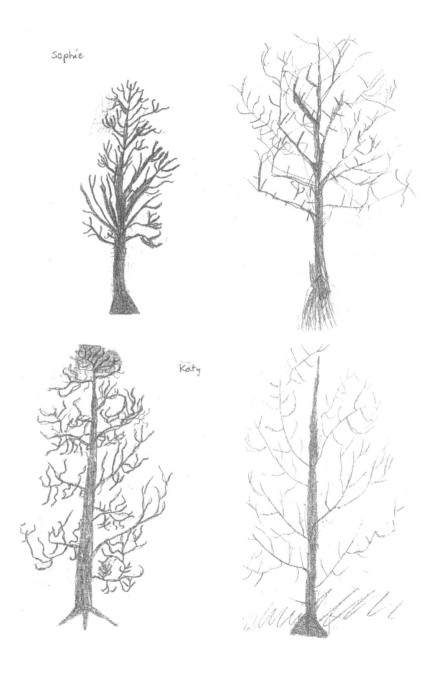

Figure 10.2: Tree drawings by Year 3

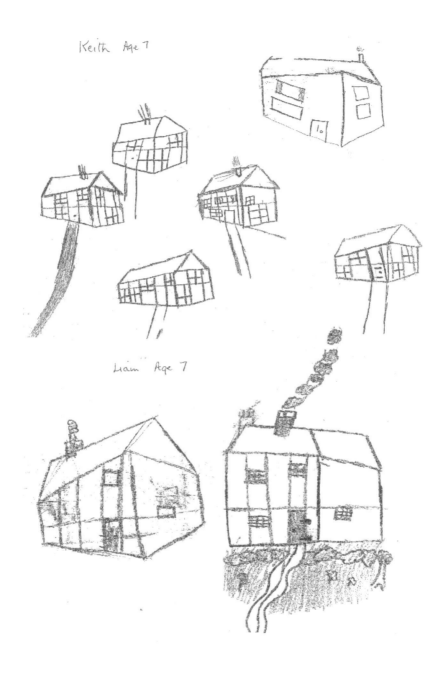

Figure 10.3: Houses by Year 3

Figure 10.4: Drawing by a Year 3 pupil

Figure 10.5: 'Me and Mum' by Year 3

Pencil and Wash. 'Henry VIII' Age 8½

by Kiera Chappell

Alex Jones

Figure 10.6: Portraits by Year 5

1st Session   Name-by sophie
              Age-7 years old

1st Guided drawing lesson

Figure 10.7: This Year 3 girl copied my wide shading when the felt-tip pen erased half its own shading on the board. Much better to use a large paper or card for demonstrating to a class (see p. 51)

Figure 10.8: First session portraits by Year 5

Figure 10.9: Basic shape drawing by Year 5

Figure 10.10: Different generations: portraits by Years 5–6

Figure 10.11: Different generations by Year 5

Figure 10.12: Historical portraits by Year 5

Figure 10.13: Portraits by Years 5–6

Conclusion:
Measuring Success

How do you know when you have succeeded as an art teacher?

There are no easy pat answers to this question, but you know you are on the right lines when you are able to tackle an art lesson with the same confidence as the other subjects which you teach and when you have established benchmarks from which your pupils can differentiate between true art and the merely 'arty'. Hopefully your children will have the confidence to start afresh at the beginning of the next lesson without having to revisit the previous session; they will be able to discuss 'modern art' dispassionately and with confidence; and they will use their imagination to produce readily recognizable shapes and forms in any media. Above all, they will work with joy and enthusiasm and know their potential as artists.

We have all been led by the nose to accept the 'experts'' opinions on what is good and what is bad. Ability to 'do art' gives the individual the right to choose for him/herself, taking the credibility from the critics and putting it back where it belongs – in the eye of the beholder!

So let us not lose the opportunity to open the children's minds to observe and criticize, the chance to evaluate the options available and develop their full potential. Show them the basics, and they will take off like rockets. By guiding them just one step further now, you are opening up their horizons. The sky is the limit!

Index